MAXIMUM SECURITY

MAXIMUM SECURITY

Karen Farrington

CHARTWELL
BOOKS, INC.

This edition printed in 2008 by
CHARTWELL BOOKS, INC.
A Division of **BOOK SALES, INC.**
114 Northfield Avenue
Edison, New Jersey 08837

ISBN-13: 978-0-7858-2388-9
ISBN-10: 0-7858-2388-3

Printed in China

CONTENTS

INTRODUCTION

A SPELL behind bars begins with the reverberating clang of a metal door, its echo evoking emotional isolation, mind-numbing monotony and a stifling atmosphere heavy with unspoken brutality. Most of us can only imagine what life in jail is like because, by and large, we live as society dictates we should. There are, however, rule-breakers in every community around the globe only too well acquainted with incarceration. Statistics show that prison populations are rising just about everywhere in the world with each passing year.

Prisons have a long and inglorious history. From Babylonian and Biblical sources we know that jail cells were used in ancient times for those accused of wrong-doing and awaiting trial or anyone who had fallen into debt. Translations from the original languages tells us that some of these were known as 'houses of detention' while others were more ominously called 'houses of chains'.

With the building of great castles came a sinister development in the story of incarceration. Dungeons were the pits in the bowels of these mighty edifices where traitors, villains and other unlucky folk were detained, sometimes indefinitely.

Other favoured places for imprisonment were towers and cellars. After the ill-fated uprising led by Bonnie Prince Charlie in 1745 some 300 of his followers were imprisoned in a single cell at Carlisle Castle. Those lucky enough to escape being trampled to death survived on drops of moisture that 'sweated' from a stone in the dungeon. Their battle to stay alive was largely futile, though, as most were ultimately executed.

From the earliest literate civilizations until the eighteenth century the principal aim of prisons was simply containment. There were no thoughts of rehabilitation and being locked up was not considered the end punishment itself – that would be determined at a later date. Indeed, many of those penned up in these harsh conditions were, after a guilty verdict at a trial, destined for the scaffold. Lesser offenders were punished by fines or floggings.

AT RISK FROM DISEASE

Prisons in England were privately owned and run for profit. Inmates were frequently put in chains because that allowed the owners to economize on security. Within cell walls there was no sanitation and disease was rife. The threat of gaol fever, an acute form of typhus, soon inspired dread in even the most law-abiding of the population. This often fatal disease spread rapidly in the overcrowded conditions through the bites of lice and fleas nesting in the clothes and bedding of most of the prison population. Symptoms began with a headache and fever, then quickly progressed to a rash of red spots, gangrene and pneumonia. A prisoner, half out of his mind with illness or motivated by revenge, would frequently propel himself out of the dock towards the presiding judge during his trial. Even if the death penalty was handed down, the judge might well be buried before the accused, the latter having infected those nearby during the course of legal proceedings.

Despite the dreadful conditions within prisons, it wasn't until the seventeenth century that the concept of punishment through imprisonment became a stated objective of incarceration. In the latter years of that century there were prisons in Rome and Florence with the declared intention of reforming erring characters by depriving them of their liberty.

PERSECUTING THE POOR

Throughout Northern Europe in the 16th century, nations sought ways of steering their booming underclass in the right direction. This was especially true in England after King Henry VIII closed the monasteries upon

Traitors Gate at the Tower of London was the traditional route by which felons entered

which many people had depended for food and shelter.

In Britain there were institutions known as 'Bridewells', where poor people could work and live under the auspices of supposedly benevolent authorities. Bridewells ran in tandem with the official prison system in which more heinous criminals were incarcerated. They took their name from Bridewell Palace, a once-grand property in London donated by King Edward VI as a home for the poor. Soon similar venues spread across the country. By 1609 local justices were subject to a £5 fine if a house of correction – where the poor could be 'as straitly kept in diet as in work' – had not been established. But conditions deteriorated at Bridewells with the introduction of flogging, pillories and other punishments for its occupants who began to include pick pockets, prostitutes and other low-grade criminals. Also, as operators sought to increase profits the level of work for those inside increased. Bridewells soon became overflow accommodation for convicted felons.

Life on the inside of both Bridewells and jails went from harsh to moderately easy depending on how much money inmates could pay the poorly paid guards in a bribe that became known as 'garnish'. Money changed hands when prisoners arrived in jail, when manacles were applied or removed and for the provision of food and water. Family visits were encouraged; if relations came bearing food the guards did not have to provide it to that inmate. Seriously poor prisoners and those with no family were in danger of starving to death. Livestock was often kept within prison or Bridewell walls to improve food supplies. Indeed, it wasn't until 1792 that dogs were banned from prison while pigs and poultry were finally prohibited in 1814.

As a final blow against freedom, prisoners acquitted of charges in court could well find themselves back behind bars again for non-payment of jailer's fees. Jailers further supplemented their income by charging an eager public for the right to view notorious outlaws in the run up to their execution, a practice that lasted until 1774.

Jail fever

After one trial, or assize, held at Oxford Castle in 1577 everyone who attended was dead within 48 hours after a man appeared in court fresh from the local prison. It was the same story in 1750 at the Old Bailey, London's premier court. Among the dead this time were the Lord Mayor, two judges, an alderman, the jury and 50 others. The source of infection was two convicts in the dock. The threat was so potent that in the eighteenth century, London's Newgate prison was demolished in an unsuccessful effort to eradicate the disease.

The notorious prison hulks were old warships anchored offshore. They contained basic living facilities for prisoners and cost the government nothing as they would otherwise have been broken up

ALL AT SEA

Through the 18th century, the prison population was rising relentlessly. In France prisoners were put to work rowing galley ships. In Britain the preference was to house prisoners in defunct ships known as hulks. By day they were forced to labour on public projects and at night they were put in irons, at the mercy of whip-wielding warders in vermin-infested quarters. By 1779, just three years after hulks were commissioned, there were serious doubts among prominent members of the government about their effectiveness, not least because escapes were frequent and successful as most were moored in busy areas. Nonetheless it wasn't until 1859 that the use of hulks as alternative prisons came to an end.

While enthusiasm for the death penalty was waning, the appetite to remove law-breakers from society remained. The idea of transporting inmates abroad seemed like a

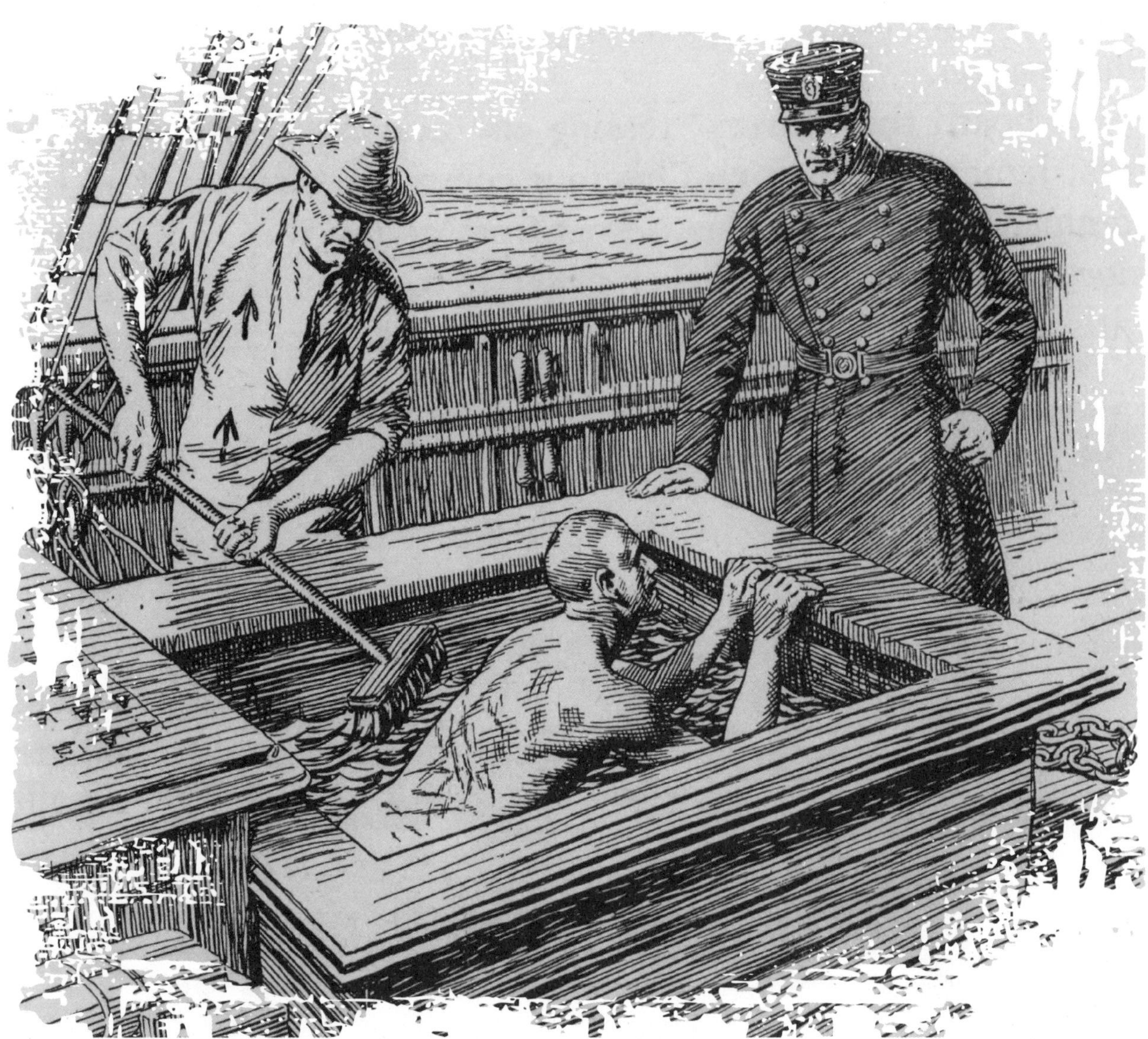

Prisons in the year 1777

Food: Many criminals are half starved: some come out almost famished, scarce able to move, and for weeks incapable of any labour.

Bedding: In many gaols, and in most Bridewells, there is no allowance of bedding or straw for prisoners to sleep on. Some lie upon rags, others upon the bare floor.

Use of Irons: Loading prisoners with heavy irons which make their walking, and even lying down to sleep, difficult and painful, is another custom which I cannot but condemn. Even the women do not escape this severity.

The Insane: At some few gaols are confined idiots and lunatics. Where these are not kept separate, they distract and terrify other prisoners.

From *The State of Prisons in England and Wales in 1777* by John Howard (1777)

perfect answer to England's dilemma. Explorers had marked out new territories across the globe ripe for exploitation and the prison population provided a workforce ready to hack a settlement out of the wilderness and willing to endure the privations and fears of the unknown. At first the destination was North America then, after 1788, inmates were sent to Australia for terms of seven or 14 years.

The first voyage to Botany Bay took 252 days. Although the 730 inmates were allowed on deck when the six transport ships were at sea, they were locked inside, sometimes for weeks at a time, while the fleet was in port. The oldest convict was Dorothy Handland, 82, who had received a seven-year sentence for perjury. Unlike 48 others, she survived the journey but hanged herself from a gum tree a year after arriving Down Under. The youngest was nine-year-old chimney sweep John Hudson, who

had been convicted of stealing some clothes and a gun.

Although transportation helped to alleviate the prison population, the conditions in English jails remained squalid.

THE SOUND OF SILENCE

John Howard (1726-1790), the eminent prison reformer who once served time in a French jail, campaigned to end the practice of warders receiving money from inmates. He suggested a different approach, advising that 'Solitude and silence are favourable to reflection and may possibly lead to repentance'.

These well-meaning words were later taken to extremes and evolved into a system of solitary and silent treatment for prisoners, with catastrophic effects on their mental health. Subsequent reformers including Elizabeth Fry (1780-1845) had their doubts about the system: 'I do not believe that a despairing or stupefied state is suitable for salvation.'

Innovations included masks or veils for prisoners, who were known by numbers rather than names. Great store was set by hard labour for felons, through which they might see the error of their ways. Large treadmills, known as shinscrapers, were installed in prisons, sometimes to grind corn or paddle water, but all too frequently to provide pointless occupation for the inmates.

Far left: After a flogging men had their backs scrubbed with sea water, an agonizing ordeal but one that helped halt infection

Left: An early 19th-century engraving shows the grief of those left behind as a convict ship sets sail. Most convicts transported to Australia never returned home

A contemporary woodcut of the prison reformer John Howard (1726-1790)

Although dubious about many aspects of the new-look prison regimes, Fry did much to enhance conditions for women and children and took her message overseas to France, Belgium, Holland, Denmark and Prussia. She was also influential in establishing the principal of female warders looking after women prisoners, which became law with the 1823 Gaol Act.

There was a widespread recognition that prison security and prisoner rehabilitation would be enhanced if inmates were separated into cells rather than inhabiting dormitories. Of course this meant considerable investment in buildings, at monumental cost.

As the nineteenth century wore on, innovation in jail reform shifted from Britain to the US where new architectural models were proving successful. Penitentiaries were built with cells radiating out from a central core from which prison warders could observe the inmates at all times without themselves being seen. Most prisons of the time were built to plans and layouts adapted from the core design.

This core design of prison layout was influenced by the so-called Panoptican design first mooted in 1787 by Utilitarian thinker Jeremy Bentham who envisioned a fully circular building which allowed the warders to see all parts of the building and allowed for no blind spots for maximum security. This model found favour in Holland, Cuba and, in one instance, the US, at Joliet, Illinois in 1919.

By the tail-end of the 19th century, incarceration had become the primary punishment for those processed through the world's legal systems. Although there was the option of the death penalty, support for the use of capital punishment for property-related crimes diminished in the nineteenth century.

The history of prisons is filled with some triumphs and numerous tragedies. Now it's time to put flesh on the bones and find out what life behind bars in the twenty-first century is all about.

In 1818, philanthropist and English MP Sir Thomas Fowell Buxton described how those awaiting trial suffered:

'The moment he enters prison irons are hammered on to him; then he is cast into the midst of a compound of all that is disgusting and depraved. At night he is locked up in a narrow cell with perhaps half a dozen of the worst thieves in London, or as many vagrants, whose rags are alive and in actual motion with vermin; he may find himself in bed and in bodily contact, between a robber and a murderer or between a man with a foul disease on one side and one with an infectious disorder on the other. He may spend his days deprived of free air and wholesome exercise . . . He may be half starved for want of food and clothing and fuel.'

Elizabeth Fry and Ann Buxton shown on their visit to the women of Newgate Prison on 15 February 1813

I

SECURITY, SOLITUDE & HARD LABOUR

PRISON populations are rising and nowhere more so than in the US where policies to get tough on crime and career criminals have resulted in mighty bulges in the jailbird fraternity.

To deal with the mushrooming number of felons America needed more jails. Those built in response to the prison population crisis were of the maximum security type and ushered in a new era of incarceration that has won enthusiastic support and entrenched criticism in almost equal measure.

The age of the Supermax has made the prison experience in America stand out on the international scene. Of course, these are probably not the worst jails in the world. There are plenty of others that are routinely more reprehensible and repulsive. But when it comes to maximum security, they are at the top of the pile. There's simply no wriggle room for inmates — and that's how the guards like it. Any notion that prison life is tinged with glamour or that prisoners bask in misplaced glory is soon eradicated. Life in a Supermax is as grim as it gets.

On 16 January 1997 two bombs were detonated at the abortion clinic in Sandy Springs near Atlanta, Georgia. The bombs were later linked to Eric Rudolph

ERIC RUDOLPH

WHEN the Olympics came to Atlanta, Georgia, a bubbling carnival atmosphere pulled in the crowds and 44-year-old Alice Hawthorne was not about to miss out on the chance to party.

'If somebody went to all the trouble to bring the Olympics to Atlanta, the least I can do is go,' the woman from Albany, Georgia, told friends.

So it was with high spirits that she and her 14 year-old-daughter, Fallon, set off on 26 July 1996 to savour the buzz of an international event.

Tragically, a visit that day to the same place by domestic terrorist Eric Rudolph ensured that this would be the last trip Alice ever made. Rudolph was not there to celebrate sporting excellence or relish a vibrant ambiance. Rather, to 'confound, anger and embarrass' the government on the abortion issue, he came armed with a vicious pipe bomb and planted it where an R & B band was playing. One moment Alice was dancing delightedly with her daughter in the early hours of 27 July, the next she lay fatally wounded from bomb shrapnel. It was the biggest pipe bomb the FBI had ever seen.

Another man, camera crew member Melih Uzunyol from Turkey, died of a heart attack as he rushed to the scene of the bombing.

Investigators mistakenly believed a security man was to blame. He was ultimately cleared of involvement but it was seven years and three bomb attacks later before Rudolph was finally arrested, scavenging for food by a store in the early morning hours.

Bombing career

Rudolph was responsible for a bomb planted at an Atlanta women's clinic on 16 January 1997 in which seven people were injured. Another bomb, which injured four at a night-club with a predominately lesbian clientele the following month, was also his work. A second bomb at the same venue failed to detonate.

An off-duty policeman died and a nurse was severely injured in an explosion outside an abortion clinic in Birmingham, Alabama on 29 January 1998. The outrage was followed up with a chilling note that read: 'The bombing in Birmingham was carried out by the Army of God. Let those who work in the murder mill's (sic) around the nation be warned once more — you will be targeted without quarter — you are not immune from retaliation. Your commissar's (sic) in Washington can't protect you.'

The Army of God is a violent offshoot of a fundamentalist group known as Christian Identity, which espouses anti-Semitic, white supremacist beliefs. Rudolph, a Catholic, was fervently anti-abortion.

In Birmingham, Rudolph's truck was identified close to the scene of the carnage and he became a prime suspect. Once that was known Rudolph vanished. It soon became clear that he was a keen survivalist and was living rough, with the help of supporters, in Nantahala National Forest in northwest North Carolina. His family shared the same extreme anti-establishment views. Indeed, after being pressured by investigators, Rudolph's younger brother Daniel protested by cutting off his hand with a radial saw while a domestic video camera rolled. The limb was later successfully re-attached.

So Rudolph, when caught, was someone with an agenda, a message to spread among society. Apart from a statement read out at sentencing, this was never broadcast. The man who once headed America's 'most wanted' list pleaded guilty to the bomb attacks in order to avoid the death penalty and he received three consecutive life terms without parole before he had an opportunity to preach extensively in the courtroom. And when he became prisoner number 18282-058 at the ADX in Florence, Colorado, he was effectively buried alive. For a man who loved living outdoors, the contrast of incarceration after years as a fugitive in the wild must have stunned the senses.

Inside Supermax

The ADX in Florence is one of two federal prisons that fall into the bracket of 'Supermax' while about 30 others are run by state authorities. It is a prison system that focuses on containment rather than rehabilitation and was established in 1983 following the death of two prison officers at the hands of inmates in separate incidents on the same day in Marion, Illinois. That prison went into permanent lock-down, which basically means putting as many bars and solid steel doors as possible between inmates and officers to keep the latter out of harm's way for the majority of the time. One of Supermax's key themes is sensory depravation and life inside it is one without

Eric Rudolph is led from Cherokee County Jail on 2 June 2003. He later pleaded guilty to the 1996 Atlanta Olympic Games bombings

stimuli as basic as seeing and touching other people or having a conversation. Other countries use solitary confinement as a punishment but it is usually in response to rule-breaking and is for a limited duration. In Supermax it is a way of life.

Opened in 1994, ADX Florence, also known as the Alcatraz of the Rockies, is the harshest of a complex of prisons built on 37 acres and has just under 500 beds. Those sent there are considered the most dangerous in the system. To kill is nothing new – they've done it before and would do so again in a heartbeat, given half a chance. At any given time it's safe to assume that a quarter of its population has murdered a fellow inmate while a third is guilty of attacking officers and inmates in ordinary jails. Only five per cent of ADX Florence's population is sent here straight from a courtroom, Rudolph among them.

What was awaiting him? A spartan cell measuring no more than 8 ft by 12 ft and containing a moulded concrete bunk, stool and desk; a steel shower, sink and toilet; and a 13 inch black-and-white TV – getting only a few channels – encased in Plexiglas so it can't be broken up or used as a weapon.

At one end of the cell there is a solid steel door and a small hallway protected by steel bars, which provides a safe haven for guards when they enter. There is one 4 in by 4 ft window. Rudolph's is over his bed, looking out on the prison yard.

Its design deprives the human faculties of any sense of normality. For example, inmates have almost no physical contact with other people. Religious services are broadcast rather than attended and visits are strictly non-contact. Food, mail and laundry are delivered through a slot in the steel bars – breakfast at 5.30am, lunch at 11am and dinner at 4pm. Prison staff sit in control booths from which they operate the doors and watch the corridors via security cameras. There are no fewer than 1,400 cameras and motion detectors to monitor. Although there's little to distinguish day from night, prisoners have complained of being woken by hourly siren 'tests' or by flashlights shone in their faces as the prison guards do their rounds.

Prisoners have a choice of two kinds of meals. One provides typical American food such as casseroles and hamburgers. The alternative is tailored to almost all religions whatever their dietary needs. It contains no pork and incorporates lots of beans and vegetables. Muslims get special mealtimes during the month of Ramadan, when adherents do not eat during daylight hours.

Rudolph is locked up alongside a number of Arab-speakers including Mahmud Abouhalima, who got 240 years without the chance of parole for his part in the 1993 World Trade Center bombing; Yemeni cleric and Al Qaeda paymaster Mohammed Ali Hassan Al-Moayad; Zacarious Moussaoui, the only man convicted following the 9/11 aircraft attacks in America; and shoe-bomber Richard Reid. Muslims are treated largely the same as other inmates but are spared body searches, although they must undergo special X rays to pinpoint foreign objects every time they re-enter their cells.

Letters home

Letters Rudolph has written to his mother, the *Colorado Springs Gazette* reporter Mary Anne Vollers give an insight into his life in lockdown.

Rudolph told *Gazette* readers that Supermax was 'a closed-off world designed to isolate inmates from social and environmental stimuli, with the ultimate purpose of causing mental illness and chronic physical conditions such as diabetes, heart disease and arthritis.'

Meanwhile, Vollers heard more about life on the inside through Rudolph's letters.

> 'It is Ramadan now and the Muslims are fasting,' Rudolph wrote three months after he arrived at ADX. 'The call to prayer echoes through the halls five times a day giving this place a decidedly otherworldly feel.'

While inmates are kept in isolation, their cells aren't soundproof so, we learn from Rudolph, the prison vibrates with noise, either the mechanical clanks of electronically-controlled cell doors or conversations via air vents in both English and Arabic.

> 'Through the slit window one can see the sky, but other than this and the few small birds that roost on the prison roof, there are no signs of the natural world.'

After a while prisoners all take on the same alabaster pallor from lack of daylight. They do have the opportunity to leave their cells but it's far from straightforward. To begin with, two guards enter the protected hallway at the end of the cell and order the inmate to strip. After a cavity search, he dresses again and his hands are encased in cuffs after he thrusts his lower arms through an opening in the bars. Only at that point will guards open the door so that they are in the same immediate vicinity as the prisoner.

Brandishing steel-tipped batons, the guards then march the prisoner down the corridor to the recreation area. When all the prisoners are lined up, they are led outdoors. Surrounded by 25ft-high walls, the area is covered with metal cages known as 'dog runs'. One prisoner is assigned to each cage. Even now the view of the sky is partially obscured by strong wire mesh.

The call to prayer echoes through the halls five times a day, giving this place a decidedly otherworldly feel

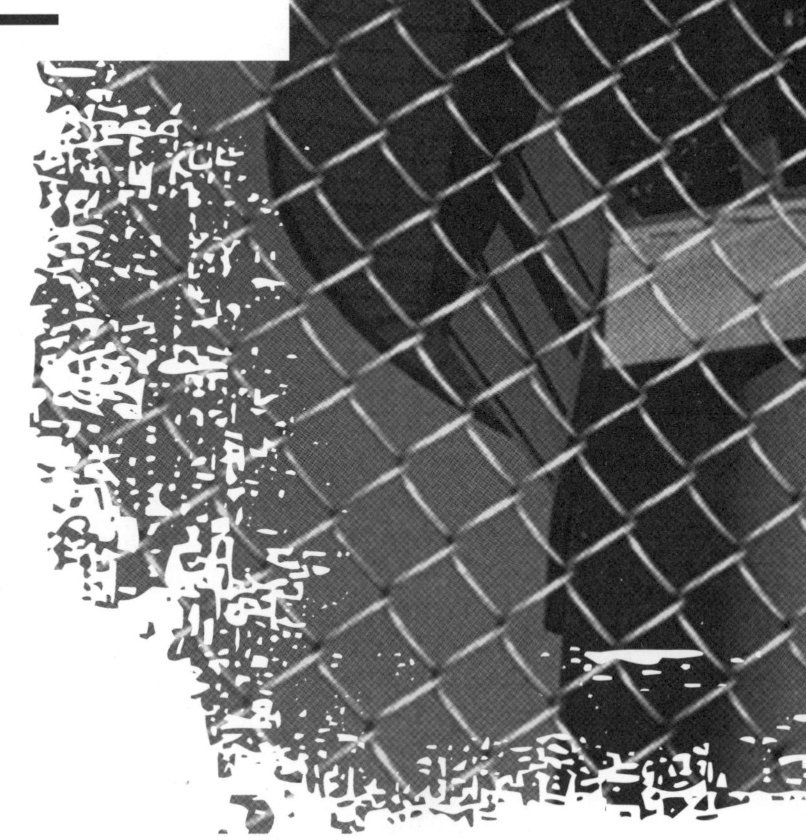

Once in the dog runs the cuffs are removed, again through a door slot. This is the only time the inmates actually see and interact with one another. 'It is awkward adjusting my voice from the necessary yell of the cell block to the face-to-face conversation in the yard,' Rudolph says. 'Unlike me, the Arabs don't adjust the volume.'

Rudolph describes how his neighbours pair up in their separate runs and then:

> 'walk the length of the cage in unison, back and forth, yelling as they go. If you've ever seen big cats at a zoo, this is what they do as well. They pace back and forth, rhythmically, like a pendulum. Across the yard, this is what one sees: seven pairs of inmates pacing together, all the while yelling in loud Arabic.'

Apart from the Arab contingent, convicts within the ADX unit include the 'Unabomber' Theodore Kaczynski and spy Robert Hanssen.

Of course, Rudolph is not the only prisoner to write about life on the inside of ADX at Florence.

A group known as the 'Committee to End Marion Lockdown' was formed in 1995 and communicated with prisoners at Florence.

Troy Hicks, prisoner number 17887-034 wrote to CEML:

A wire mesh fence surrounds a watch tower at the ADX Supermax Prison in Florence, Colorado

'We have boredom, tedium, depression, sadness, or simply the blues of sensory deprivation and mental stagnation from 23 hours a day of confinement. In most cases, prisoners are merely looking at a blank wall or the steel bars with no conception or pictures of the voice he is hearing entombed with him 23 hours a day. This sometimes creates psychopathic emotional distress, memory loss and déjà

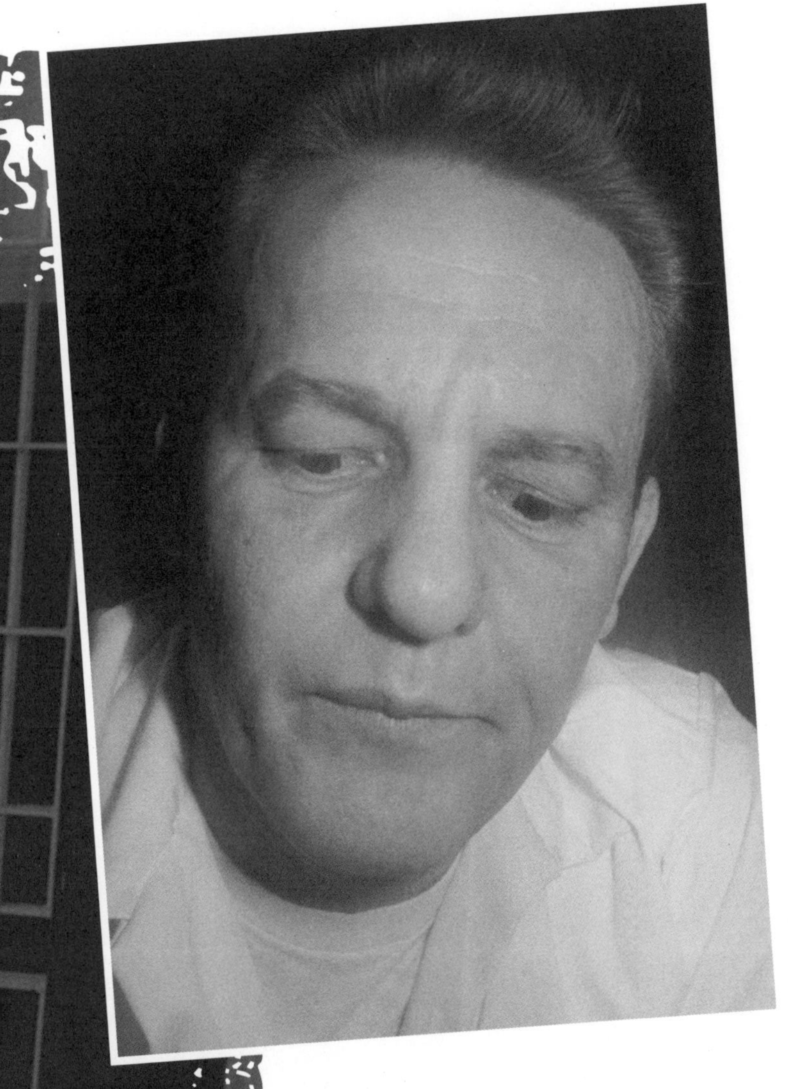

vu, for surely this is the twilight zone.'

Meanwhile another Supermax inmate, Woody Raymer, prisoner number 09346-074 told CEML:

'You asked me to comment about Florence ADX, and I shall do so, even though I'm not sure I know the words which can adequately explain some of my feelings and opinions. I doubt seriously if the words exist which can truly portray the deep feelings of loneliness, depression, degradation, alienation, and despair which I've experienced in only seven months of being caged in Florence ADX. I speak my feelings, regardless of the reprisals that are sure to come, even if they're indirect. My mind, soul, and body have become numb to harassment, ridicule, censorship, broken promises and nothingness.

'In court, a person found guilty of a crime is sentenced to serve time in a prison, and their physical freedom is lost. The sentence and the loss of freedom is their punishment and they aren't supposed to be punished again while in prison, month after month, year after year, in the most abject manner.'

Prison killing

Although Supermax prisons are designed primarily to keep staff safe, prison welfare is also an issue. Attacks by inmates on fellow prisoners are common in regular jails but almost eliminated in Supermax. However, a startling killing on the inside of ADX Florence revealed the system was far from infallible.

Saipanese cousins William and Rudy Sablan murdered a fellow prisoner named Joey Jesus Estrella in a holding cell designed for prisoners who need protection from other prisoners or those who have violated prison rules.

First, Estrella was strangled with a headphone cord then his throat was slit with a plastic razor and his stomach split open. William Sablan brandished Estrella's internal organs to guards as they took stock of the blood-soaked scene.

It has been alleged, though without any real evidence, that Estrella was a gang member who was drunk on home-made hooch at the time of his death.

William Sablan was subsequently convicted of the murder of Estrella and sentenced to life with no chance of parole. He was spared the death penalty as the jury's verdict was not unanimous. As this book went to press, Rudi Sablan still awaited trial.

Left: The interior of a typical cell at the ADX Supermax Prison at Florence. One of its more famous inmates, Charles Harrelson (inset), father of US actor Woody Harrelson, died there of natural causes in March 2007

Boscobel, USA

'THE TOUGHEST OF THE TOUGH'

It's the town where the goodly notion of Gideon's Bibles was conceived and the capital of wild turkey hunting. But now Boscobel, Wisconsin, population 3,000, is famous for something altogether more malignant and malevolent. It's the site of a Supermax, probably the harshest prison regime in the Western world

LOCAL POLITICIANS heralded the arrival of the Supermax by crowing that it was not a jail for ordinary offenders but one to house 'the toughest of the tough, the real bad actors'. Local people responded by banding together to raise the necessary cash for the land purchase.

Today no one gets sent to Boscobel from a courthouse dock after a jury verdict. It's designed for those men who have attacked wardens or other inmates in state prisons, who push the boundaries of prison routine to the breaking point or beyond.

Low and almost square, it crouches in some of America's most hospitable countryside. Before prisoners arrived for the first time in November 1999 there was a six-day open house during which vendors sold sodas, sausages and T-shirts. Tens of thousands of people, including some 3,000 schoolchildren, were bussed in from around the state and toured the facility. According to press accounts, some visitors were angered to see TVs in cells, believing it was one luxury too far. Prisoners, however, would beg to differ for life at Boscobel is the ultimate no-frills existence.

Big five for the first timers

When they arrive for the first time, prisoners are greeted by white-shirted officers who escort them to a strip cell for an intrusive full-body search. Then it's off to Alpha unit with eyes facing forward. Here the prisoners say farewell to personal belongings and learn what lies ahead – a period of solitary confinement of uncertain duration.

There are five levels of discipline and each prisoner begins at level one. This means he is locked in a small, windowless cell at all times except for four hours a week of recreation and exercise that are undertaken with uncomfortable restraints binding the hands. The cell has a stainless steel toilet and sink and a mattress softens the concrete slab – the bed.

For an inmate on level one there's no television, radio, clock or watch. In fact, the only electronic device in the room is the security camera that rolls 24/7. Prisoners are forbidden to tape anything to the walls. There's no book provision either, although inmates are allowed one religious text, a box of legal documents and 25 personal letters.

The lights stay on around the clock, ostensibly so guards can make observational checks through the door hatches at any time. Prisoners must sleep with skin showing for the benefit of inspection by guards and anyone who has covered his face at night is woken from slumber to reorganize the bedclothes. In the summer the temperature in the cells can soar to more than 100 degrees Fahrenheit for, of course, there's no air conditioning. In the winter it is freezing. Provisions that can be bought from the canteen are strictly limited. Prisoners receiving meals through the door hatch must be standing in the middle of the cells and dressed in at least their trousers when it arrives or they are deemed to have refused food.

Telephone calls are limited to one a month, lasting for six minutes only. Apart from lawyer consultation, 'visits' are via a video link. That means that although friends and family might make a costly and time-consuming trip to Boscobel they will only see their loved one on a screen, never in the flesh.

All fixtures and fittings in the canteen of an ADX Supermax Prison are screwed firmly to the floor to prevent their use as weapons

A cell at an ADX Supermax Prison includes basic furnishings, but nothing that could be used as a weapon or escape tool

District Judge Barbara Crabb described conditions at Boscobel in a 2001 ruling: 'Because of the heavy walls and boxcar doors at Supermax there is a constant muffled sound broken intermittently by loud yells and slamming gates. A five-inch strip of opaque glass runs along the top edge of one wall of each cell. By standing on the bed and craning his neck an inmate can glimpse the sky through a small, sealed skylight.'

If prisoners survive for the required 30 days at level one without committing a misdemeanour, they are elevated to level two. Accommodation remains the same but now there is the opportunity to make two six-minute telephone calls every month plus the added attraction of library privileges. After 90 days there's the chance to hit level three where a TV is provided, albeit one with access to only four educational channels. The telephone entitlement is increased to two 12-minute calls a month and the choice of canteen food is enhanced. It is six months before prisoners can reach level four and a further 90 days before they are eligible for level five, where an in-cell hobby is allowed. Only then will prisoners be eligible for transfer to an ordinary jail, having proved some measure of rehabilitation.

Prisoners can move down security levels as well as up. One man was reduced for not returning a library book on time, another for screening off the in-cell camera while he used the toilet. At no time in Boscobel are prisoners

permitted communal activities although illicit communication occurs through air vents.

'I'd rather be hit by a truck'

Perhaps unsurprisingly, prisoners are critical of the regime. 'Most of the time I wished to die. The boredom and hopelessness is appalling. At least on the street a truck could hit you. At Boscobel, the best I could hope for was to contract a terminal disease,' said one inmate. Another continues:

> 'Millions of dollars have been spent to put cameras in these one-man segregation cells. For what purpose? To catch people eating granola bars that they save from breakfast? To watch them urinate, defecate, shower and masturbate? WI Supermax is one big peepshow. There's no way to escape these cells or the cameras. Obviously the DOC [Department of Correction] is not worried about security because on three occasions already the high-priced electronic doors have malfunctioned and opened the wrong cell doors, with prisoners inside. Fifty per cent of the guys are here because sometime in the last 10 years they got into a fist fight with another prisoner, or for no reason at all. One guy was here because he enclosed a letter to his mother with another letter. I got into more fist fights in high school than I have in prison. Hockey players get into fist fights all the time and it's merely an entertaining diversion.
>
> The politicians have lied to you. There is no "worst of the worst" in Wisconsin. Every prison has its own segregation complex to deal with rule infractions. I've been in Supermax for over two years for a fist fight in which I threw one punch.'

But the authorities are unmoved. During a visit in 2001, state governor 'Tommy' Thompson, who fought to have the prison sited at Boscobel, was satisfied with what he found. 'It's accomplishing its purpose. The toughest of the tough, the worst elements of our prison society are in this institution. They're in here because of their behavior and they can get out because of their behaviour. They don't like being here but they are not being abused in any way. None of their civil rights are being adversely affected. They would like to be outside and I can agree with them. So would I.'

AWESOME REPUTATION

Supermaxes are expensive to run, with meals being indivually delivered and multiple guards needed for escort duties. While the cost of keeping a prisoner in a Supermax is about twice what it would be in a normal prison, many people think it is value for money. It offers the rarified atmosphere that many people think is appropriate for prisoners and there is simply no chance of escape.

Opportunities for self harm or prisoner attacks are likewise limited. However, it seems that the reputation of Boscobel was sufficient to inspire one man destined for the Supermax to commit suicide. Before hanging himself in his cell, David Hatch, an inmate at the Racine Correctional Institution, left a poignant note saying: 'I told you I wasn't going to go there.'

Hatch was convicted of two counts of attempted murder after an incident in 1985 in which he shot his estranged girlfriend, a police officer and himself – all in the head. The police officer stayed in a coma until his death some years later.

Milwaukee Circuit Reserve Judge Fred Kessler presided over Hatch's trial in Beloit and thought him 'a real bad guy.' Yet he was horrified to hear of the suicide. 'I was reminded of Devil's Island,' he says of the fearsome Supermax. 'It starts to cross over into cruel and unusual punishment, and it reflects badly on society.'

An estimated 20,000 people are incarcerated in America's Supermax facilities and all wrestle with the same psychological demands in a system dubbed 'no-touch torture'.

After a tour of Texas' high security blocks in 1999 Dr Craig Haney was asked what stood out most about his visits:

'The bedlam which ensued each time I walked out into one of those units; the number of people who were screaming, who were begging for help, for attention; the number of people who appeared to be disturbed; the existence, again, of people who were smeared with feces; the intensity of the noise as people began to shout and ask, 'Please come over here. Please talk to me. Please help me.' It was shattering. And as I discussed this atmosphere with the people who worked here I was told that this was an everyday occurrence, that there was nothing at all unusual about what I was seeing.'

The sound of silence

It's not the first time prisoners have been kept in solitude in US prisons. In fact, as a young nation America was a trail blazer in terms of jail-house reform and the brave new world of punishment introduced back then centred on solitary conditions. Out went whipping posts, stocks and branding irons, strongly associated with colonial Britain. The mayhem that once overwhelmed prisons was brought under control in the form of two systems that were deemed both civilized and reformative.

There was the Pennsylvanian system in which prisoners were taken to their cells in blindfolds and kept there in silence and isolation for the duration of their sentence. The most famous prisons constructed for this system were the Eastern State Penitentiary at Cherry Hill, Philadelphia, built in 1829, and the Western Pennsylvania Prison in Pittsburgh, constructed in 1882. Prisoners were given modern facilities in their cells – the jailhouse at Cherry Hill was probably the nation's first building with indoor plumbing – and a Bible to read. Excluded entirely from communal living, the prisoners worked at crafts like shoe-mending or candle-making in their cells and the presumption was that temptation to break rules was entirely removed. Those in charge congratulated themselves on devising a humane, ordered system of incarceration. But the effect was at times catastrophic.

After the system was tried in New York in 1821, there was a sharp increase in the instances of death and insanity. One man who burst out of his cell when the door was opened leapt from the fourth-floor corridor in an attempt to kill himself, surviving only because a pipe broke his fall. Another inmate, according to a report at the time, 'beat and mangled his head against the walls of his cell, destroying one of his eyes.' Following a high level inspection two years later, most of those who remained part of the experiment were pardoned. The results proved that 20 months in solitary had done nothing to help them reform. Twelve of the men who were pardoned were soon back with new convictions, including one who committed a burglary near the prison the night after his release. Writer Charles Dickens paid a visit in 1842 and wrote that 'the slow and daily tampering with the mysteries of the brain was... immeasurably worse than any torture to the body.'

There's a lot of faeces-flinging in Supermax establishments. When excrement is mixed with urine, the substance is known as Agent Orange. Prison guards often wear eye goggles for protection

By the turn of the century the taste for the Pennsylvanian system had largely been lost – not least because prisoners working alone in cells were less productive than those working communally – although the design of penitentiaries intended for its use, with corridors radiating from a hub, found favour.

The Auburn system was likewise silent and prisoners were kept singly in cells. However, they ate and worked together, albeit without talking. Prison officials could survey their charges via a 2,000-foot passageway behind the workshops, with narrow slits for peep-holes. The same passageway was also a tourist attraction and some 6,000 people a year paid 25 cents admission, with a guidebook available for another 25 cents.

Auburn prison, which opened in 1825, had 55 single cells measuring seven and a half ft by three ft eight in and was intended for the most violent offenders. Prisoners considered less dangerous were put in solitary confinement for three days each week. Inmates had shaved heads and wore distinctive black and white uniforms.

The 'no talking' rule was taken seriously as it was intended that criminals should contemplate their crimes and find the mental capacity to reform. So the air was always thick with silence. Although they couldn't 'talk the talk' they were compelled to 'walk the walk'. At Auburn prisoners moved in a lockstep, with one hand on the shoulder of the man in front and their heads to the right so that the prison guards could watch for lip movement. Obviously, whispered or signed conversations occured, as did the development of a finger alphabet, despite the prospect of an instant flogging for anyone found illicitly communicating.

In fact, when prisoners broke the rules by talking through ventilation ducts they could barely be heard because the cell walls were so thick. In 1831 the political thinker and historian Alexis de Tocqueville (1805-59) reported that in Auburn 'everything passes in the most profound silence, and nothing is heard in the whole prison but the steps of those who march, or sounds proceeding from the workshops. But when the day is finished, and the prisoners have retired to their cells, the silence within these vast walls...is that of death. We have often trod at night those monotonous and dumb galleries, where a lamp is always burning; we felt as if we traversed catacombs; there were a thousand living beings, and yet it was a desert solitude.'

Before the end of the nineteenth century the silent systems were discarded for many decades. Solitary confinement still existed in the form of 'the hole', a cell or section where prisoners were punished for a specific misdemeanour for a limited duration.

Solitary confinement

When prison systems based on isolation and imposed silence returned in the guise of the Supermax some of the initial reasons for their inception back in the nineteenth century still held good. Silent and segregated prisoners could not hatch escape plans or co-ordinate attacks on prison guards, nor could they school incomers in crime. The inability of prisoners to communicate unhindered gives prison guards the upper hand on a day-to-day basis. And with the Supermax, isolation has been honed to a fine art.

Dr. Craig Haney, an expert in prison psychology explains its 'refinement'.

> 'Solitary confinement has been around for a long time. What's different about these Supermax units is that the technology of the modern correctional institution allows for a separation, almost a technological separation, of inmates from the social world around them in ways that weren't really possible in the past.'

Scientific tests on brain waves have proved that solitary confinement quickly produces 'stupor and delirium' and certainly some Supermax prisoners respond badly to the closeted environment. One recurring dilemma is self-mutilation among inmates. Experts claim that the motivation for bodily slashers and hackers is a twisted sense of self validation and the need to prompt a reaction, even if it's a brutal one.

At Arizona's Supermax Special Management Unit H, one inmate castrated himself with an eating utensil and another tried to gouge out an eyeball with a pencil. At the new Supermax in Tamms, Illinois, an inmate carved into his own flesh and ate scraps of the bloody tissue, then ripped out the sutures and rubbed excrement into the reopened wounds.

Agent Orange

There's a lot of faeces-flinging in Supermax establishments. When excrement is mixed with urine the substance is known as Agent Orange. Prison guards often wear eye goggles for protection.

An Agent Orange attack is a common phenomenon because men who have lost control over every other aspect of their lives choose this base method to make a low-grade

Solitary confinement can induce torpor, listlessness and a number of other psychological problems

statement of independence. Prison psychiatrists admit they are frequently at a loss to know whether it is a sign of mental illness or simply bad behaviour.

Dr. Stuart Grassian has interviewed numerous prisoners to study the possible effects of solitary confinement. He has compiled a list of symptoms suffered by men kept in isolation. These include hearing voices, including whispers; an inability to tolerate noise – even background sounds like plumbing; panic attacks; an inability to concentrate and memory blips; aggressive fantasies of revenge, torture and mutilation of the guards; paranoia; self doubt; difficulty determining what is real; and problems controlling impulses which can sometimes lead to acts of random violence.

Women as well as men are subject to Supermax-style sentences, usually carried out in a jail wing. One woman, who refused to be named, told the San Francisco Chronicle:

> 'I feel like I have been shattered into a million little pieces. The threats of violence, the constant sexual abuse [allegedly from prison guards], the complete powerlessness that I experienced in an abusive relationship were still in my life, only in the SHU (Security Housing Unit) it's the state that is doing it.'

She had been sentenced to 11 years for killing a violent partner. But if she thought being separated from her four children was punishment enough she was wrong.

Felonies like spitting at prison officers got her thrown into lockdown and she received a further 24-year sentence for her defiant gestures. Only frantic work by her legal team reduced the sentence to manageable proportions.

> 'In the SHU I felt like they were trying to take away part of my identity,' she said. 'Your sense of creativity gets lost, your sense of identity gets lost. All I could do was try to hold on to those fundamental things. I was fighting so hard just to hang on to a sense of self.'

A solitary cell at the Pelican Bay State Prison, California. Such cells are usually reserved for violent gang members

Tight fit in the SHU

California's Pelican Bay prison lies just eleven miles from the Oregon border in 275 acres of remote countryside. Opened in 1989 at a cost of some $220 million, it is now home to 3,400 inmates, significantly more than it was intended to house.

Apart from a general prison population it has a Security Housing Unit (SHU) with cells

built in an X-shape. Inside the SHU the individual cells are antiseptic white and without windows. Before prisoners enter, their clothing, belongings and bedding are X-rayed to ensure nothing untoward is taken inside. Radios and televisions are allowed but may be taken away following rule infringements.

Phone calls are forbidden and prisoners may receive only one parcel from home per year. They are separated from loved ones during visits by a transparent shield and must talk via a telephone. In fact, the location of Pelican Bay – hundreds of miles from the cities that most inmates call home – means the number of visitors is severely curtailed.

Prison psychiatrist Terry Kupers explains the Pelican Bay effect:

> 'It's a very eerie scene up in Pelican Bay. I first went up there in the early 1990s. Pelican Bay was like a bunker. You're driving through the forest and then you come to a clearing, and there are white rocks all around it and there's this concrete bunker. It's bizarre. It feels like a spaceship just landed in the forest. There's such sterility inside and such greenery and beauty outside, which the prisoners can't see.'

Conditions at Pelican Bay Supermax got better in 1995 after a judge ordered improvements in health care for prisoners and questioned the level of force used by some prison officers. He ordered all prisoners suffering mental health problems to be removed from the institution.

Despite the tight control on its population, Pelican Bay is bustling with all sorts of activity. 'This is a city,' explains Warden Joe McGrath. 'We have our own waterworks, our own water treatment facility, we have boiler plants, we have generators to run electrical systems, we have a full medical department with hundreds of medical staff, a full education department with teachers. I have my own school district superintendent here. It goes on and on and on.'

JAILHOUSE ROT

Supermax may be the most secure jail accommodation in the US but it is not the only kind. There are hundreds of other prisons across the country, run by federal, state or local government, which cater for different security levels.

From the prisoner point of view, conditions are much worse in some than others. Few are less appealing than the prison system run by Sheriff Joe Arpaio. The sheriff, elected as law enforcer in Maricopa County, Arizona, in 1992, has started male and female chain gangs, cut food rations and introduced pink underpants for male prisoners.

Arizona's Sheriff Joe Arpaio photographed on the day he introduced the first female chain gang

None of the 8,000 prisoners in his charge receive coffee, cigarettes, salt and pepper, ketchup or recreation. Arpaio proudly points out that he has reduced inmates to two meals a day, totalling 2,500 calories, and that it costs more to feed the prison dogs than it does the prisoners. If they want medical attention prisoners must pay ten dollars. If they want to write home they must use a postcard bearing a picture of Sheriff Arpaio.

A vast swathe of prisoners who are not considered escape risks have been moved into tents in the desert. Predictably, life under canvas is uncomfortably hot. To inmates who complain Sheriff Arpaio's message is simple: 'It's 120 degrees Farenheit in Iraq and the soldiers are living in tents and they didn't commit any crimes.'

Despite condemnation from human rights activists, he woos the popular vote by being relentlessly 'tough on crime'. Media coverage of his activities has been extensive following his proclamation that there was 'nothing to hide and nothing to fear'.

Life on the inside of an Arpaio jail was revealed by the internet blog of Shaun Attwood, an Englishman found guilty in 2004 of money laundering and drugs charges after he organized raves around Phoenix.

He has catalogued conditions at Arpaio's prisons and it makes for uncomfortable reading. He says prison food was merely a

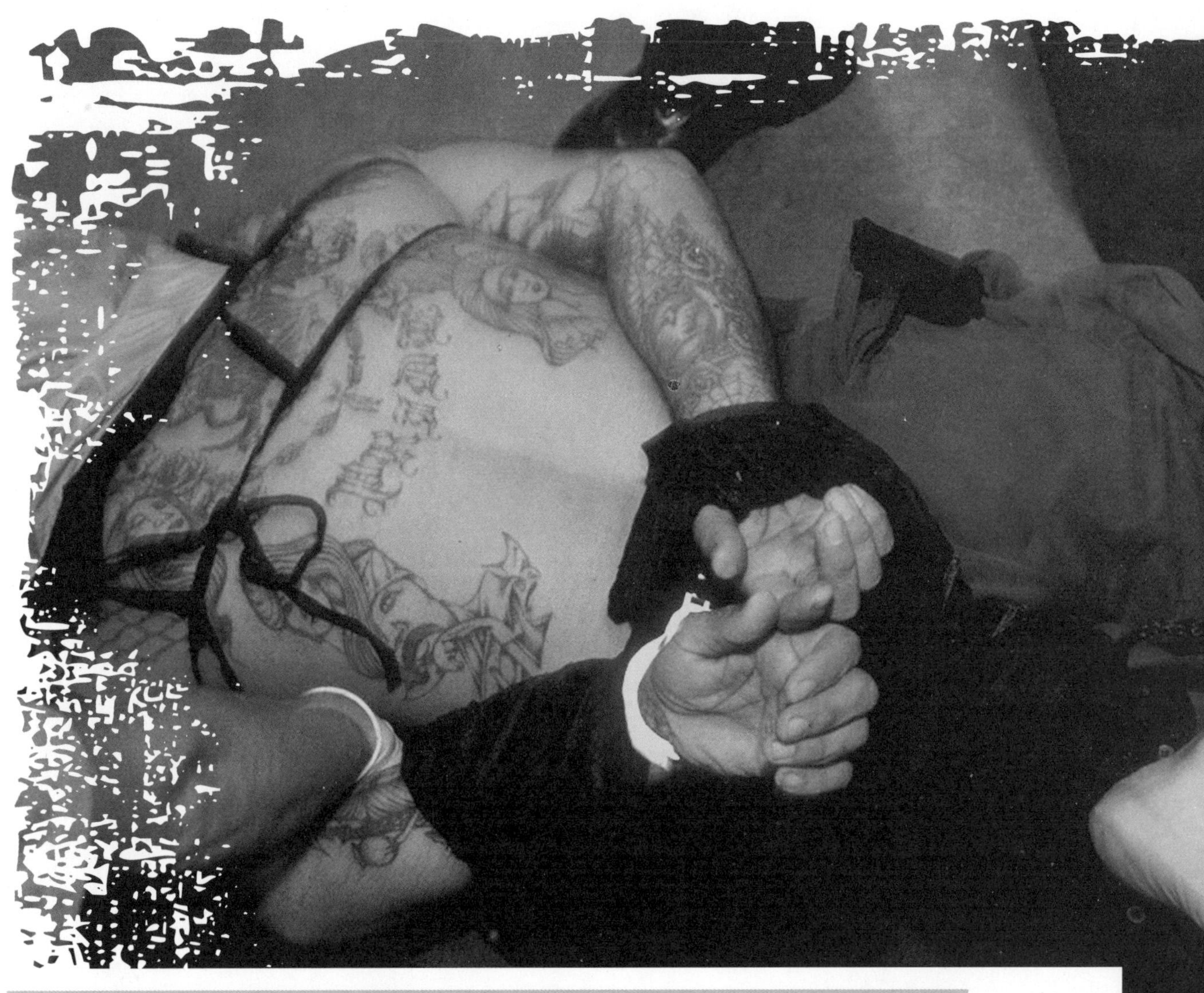

Men are over 8 times more likely than women to be incarcerated in prison at least once during their life
— U.S. Dept of Justice

mixture of rotten meat, fruit and vegetables and mouldy bread. He even says he saw a rat's head in one stew. With temperatures frequently soaring above 100 degrees Farenheit, he wrote on paper that was soaked in sweat with a pencil filed down to tiny dimensions so it could not be used as a weapon.

When the letters he wrote reached his family they were uploaded onto the internet, initially under the pseudonym of John's Jail Diary, adopted to avoid reprisals. One diary extract reveals the degradation prisoners lived in:

Diary: March 18 2004

One of the unsettling things about cellular living is that the jail authorities can randomly uproot an inmate at any time and transplant him into a new environment. During my two-year stay at the jail, I have been rolled-up (moved) several times. A new cell equals a new garrison of cockroaches to battle and I have learned to travel armed with AmerFresh Fluoride toothpaste,

Johnny Cash: Prison Hero

Country singer Johnny Cash (1932–2003) became popular with America's prison inmates for his vocal support of the underprivileged and his renegade ways. Although he never received a prison sentence – he spent seven single nights in jail and received a suspended sentence for a drugs offence – he was a hero to many behind bars. A series of concerts given at penitentiaries including Folsom Prison, in 1968, and San Quentin, in 1969, confirmed his iconic status. He also performed at Osteraker Prison in Sweden. After Cash was cured of an addiction to prescription drugs he reaffirmed his Christian faith and began campaigning for better conditions in prisons.

San Quentin, I hate every inch of you.
You've cut me and have scarred me
thru an' thru.
And I'll walk out a wiser weaker man;
Mister Congressman why can't you understand.

Johnny Cash, San Quentin

which blocks cockroach entry points very effectively.

On Tuesday our whole pod was moved to a different floor and I used my entire stock of AmerFresh to seal the numerous cockroach-launching points. The cell was quickly fortified against the enemy. That night I slept soundly. Little did I know that the jail was about to sabotage my work.

On Wednesday I was moved back to my original floor and into one of the most cockroach-infested pods in the building. I was completely unarmed and helplessly watched the insects size me up from myriad cracks in the walls. The lights were still on, but I knew that by night time I would be doomed. My new cellmate and I didn't get much sleep, but lay awake watching the legions of cockroaches conquer the room. Whirling around us, they swarmed the floor, the walls, the ceiling, our commissary bags and, finally, our bunks.

Far left: A modern take on the straitjacket; so-called 'tent-prisons' are used in some prisons to restrain inmates

A female chain gang sets out from a prison in Arizona for a day's work in the desert

Chain reaction

ARPAIO is unabashed by criticism. If time spent in jail is loathsome then men and women will go the extra mile to make sure they don't return, he reasons. His message to complaining inmates is simple: 'If you don't like it, don't come back.'

On 19 September 1996 the first-ever female chain gang took to the streets under the watchful eye of Arpaio and his men. Shackled with leg chains, they were marched to a prison van and then driven to their workplace. Usually it's a desert cemetery where they dig graves for the poor, the homeless and the nameless plus the babies that are buried weekly by the state. In addition, they paint kerbstones, tackle graffiti and pick up litter. It's all done in full view of passing motorists, many of whom honk their horns appreciatively.

According to Arpaio, the female chain gang has saved tax payers some $500,000 over three years and it gives those involved a chance to regain their self respect through hard labour.

Participation in the chain gang is voluntary. While human rights activists squabble with Arpaio about the legitimacy of the scheme the

real reasons that women prisoners choose to step out in shackles remains obscure. Some of the reasons given include:

❑ For many it is a stepping stone out of solitary confinement or 23-hour-a-day lockdown.

❑ The lunches given to chain gang members are generally better quality than food distributed inside jail.

❑ Outdoor tasks are more palatable than jail duties.

❑ Physical labour, like a gym session, helps to tone the figure.

❑ Prisoners are provided with gloves that protect their nails and any recently added hand and wrist tattoos.

❑ It makes a change.

There are also chain gangs at work in Alabama and Florida. Chain gangs have a protracted and ignominious history in America. They were created at the turn of the twentieth century, partly to fill the gap left when slavery was outlawed.

The public perception of chain gangs was altered by the memoirs of a man who twice fled from one. First World War veteran Robert Elliot Burns (1882-1955) robbed an Atlanta store in 1922 with a few other men after falling on hard times. The total take from the crime amounted to five dollars and eighty cents. Despite the poor return on the crime, Burns received a sentence of six to ten years on a chain gang.

Prisoners, including the slightly-built Burns, were taken to a quarry at 5 am wearing the familiar stripped uniforms and attached to one another by 20lb chains to begin a fifteen hour day on the awesome task of breaking stones into gravel by musclepower alone. While the sun burnt their backs, prisoners had to wield sledgehammers rhythmically under the eagle eye of sadistic guards.

'One was never allowed to rest a moment but must always be hard at work,' Burns later wrote, 'and even moving in the mass of chain was painful and tiring — yet if one did not keep up his work greater terrors and more brutal punishment was in reserve.

'If a convict wanted to stop for a second to wipe the sweat off his face, he would have to call out "Wiping it off" and wait until the guard replied, "Wipe it off" before he could do so.'

The prisoner perceived to have done the least work each day was selected by the guards for a whipping.

In desperation, Burns risked terrible injury and asked a fellow prisoner to bring the hammer down on his ankle chain, turning it from a hoop to an oval shape so that he could slip it off. He set off through a swamp at speed, ultimately shaking off the baying bloodhounds sent after him.

Burns ended up in Chicago and became a successful magazine publisher under an assumed name. However, his wife informed police of his penal history when she found out he was having an affair. In 1930 he was sent back to the chain gang, escaping a second time when he bribed a farmer.

Two years later he produced his book *I am a Fugitive from a Georgia Chain Gang*, which was soon made into a landmark film, one that would define the image of southern sheriffs as knuckle-headed and witless for decades to come. Attempts to send him back to Georgia a third time came to nothing. Burns was finally pardoned and died believing he had sounded the death knell for the chain gang. In fact, it wasn't until the 1960s before the system finally disappeared, only to re-emerge thirty years later.

'One was never allowed to rest a moment, but must always be hard at work. If one did not keep up his work, greater terrors and more brutal punishments was in reserve.'

RUSSIA

GULAGS AND YOUNG LAGS

Putting convicts to work is a common characteristic of prisons worldwide. When oil tycoon Mikhail B. Khodorkovsky was jailed for eight years on charges of tax evasion and fraud he found himself confined to a sweat-shop for 10 hours a day, making protective clothing for the prison service and police force. Previously, when his company, Yukos, was pumping more barrels of oil a day than Kuwait, Khodorkovsky was worth $8 billion. Now he was earning just over 20 roubles a day.

The task at hand was not so bad as far as physical labour was concerned. However, the fact that the prison he was sent to was IK-10 in Siberia, some 3,774 miles east of Moscow and 400 miles from the nearest city, Chita, made life considerably worse.

By train from his former home in Moscow the journey takes 106 hours and ends with a

20 km taxi ride. Alternatively, it is possible to take a six-hour flight followed by a seven-hour trek along some of the continent's most treacherous roads.

IK-10, in Krasnokamensk, previously one of Stalin's gulags, lies close to Russia's borders with both China and Mongolia.

Years ago inmates were forced to work in the nearby uranium mines and processing plant. If the hard labour didn't cut short their lives then the bitter cold surely would – although it is sweltering hot in the summer, the temperature during the winter can plummet to minus 33 degrees Celcius. And this is before the effects of uranium have the opportunity to take root.

Today conditions are generally acknowledged to be less brutal. In addition to sewing rooms, there's a car repair shop and a carpentry section. Prisoners sleep in bunks in brick dormitories that hold about 80 people. With a total population of some 1,000, the average age of inmates is 24 and most have been jailed for theft.

'It is a normal camp providing normal living conditions,' Alexander Pleshkov, head of the local prison administration, told the press.

Prisoners may well be able to survive on a breakfast of porridge or bread and boiled potatoes followed by meals lacking in fruit, fish and eggs, and with only tiny amounts of meat. However, the high levels of radioactive material that have seeped into the water table from the nearby mine and have been detected in the wells that serve the prison are a different matter. Some campaigners have branded the area an 'environmental catastrophe' and life expectancy here stands at a mere 42 years.

Khordorkovsky has been put into solitary confinement at least three times, once for drinking tea in the wrong place. On another occasion he was isolated for unauthorized possession of two lemons. He has also been slashed by another prisoner; the circumstances of the attack are largely unknown.

He is allowed just four visits a year from his family, and it is unlikely they could make the exhausting journey more frequently. His lawyers are challenging the venue of his incarceration as Russian law favours home-region imprisonment for criminals.

During his incarceration he is apparently spending his spare time helping other, often illiterate, prisoners write home, and working on a PhD dissertation.

IK-10 is rated a medium-security prison. Khodorkovsky's co-accused, Platon Lebedev, who was also found guilty in 2005 on tax evasion charges and received the same sentence, was dispatched to IK-3, a maximum-security prison notorious for violence, prisoner neglect, torture and killings.

It is located at Kharp, a village above the Arctic circle in a region known in the local dialect as 'the end of the world'. It is 1,193 miles from Moscow and in the depths of winter the temperature can register as low as minus 50 degrees C. Indeed, it is so dangerously cold that inmates must remain inside prison buildings and do not set foot in the open air for weeks at a time.

KENYA

HOT SHOTS

Meanwhile, in Kenya's Nairobi prison the problem is extreme heat. Severe overcrowding at the prison means that inmates kept at close quarters are bathed in sweat day and night.

Population statistics for Kenya's prisons in general and Nairobi prison in particular are astonishing. In 2000 there were 41,211 prisoners nationwide crammed into accommodation designed for just 18,953.

Three years later there were 3,800 prisoners within the walls of Nairobi's jail when it was built to contain just 800. A BBC correspondent found 12 inmates in a cell meant for three. They had two mattresses and no blankets. Some 250 men serving short sentences were crammed into one room with space for just 50 – and only five mattresses.

'This is the worst prison I have ever seen,' said Nigerian inmate Colin Alexander. 'Everything about this place is bad, including the treatment from the wardens. We are surviving by the grace of God.'

The budget is pitifully small: just 30 cents per head per day is set aside to provide for the prisoner. This means they have a diet of cold porridge for breakfast, *ugali* (maize meal)

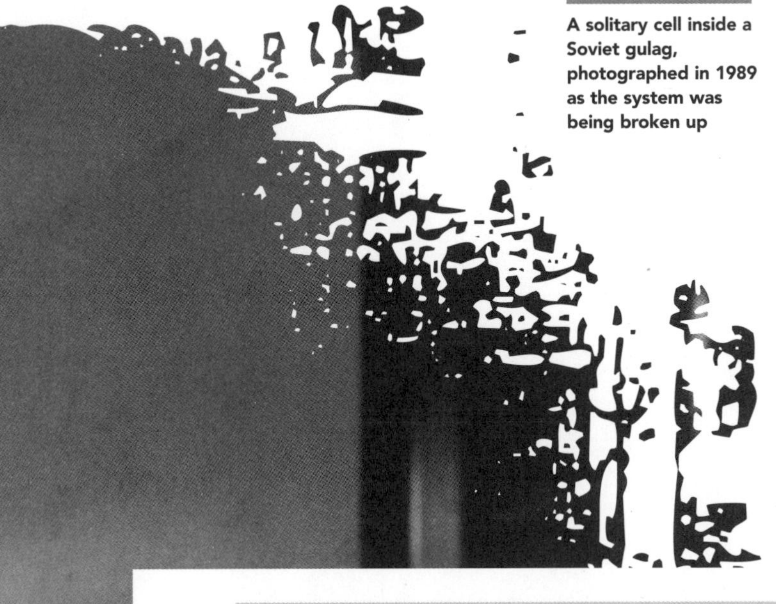

A solitary cell inside a Soviet gulag, photographed in 1989 as the system was being broken up

with greens for lunch and ugali with beans at supper time.

The stench inside the prison is stomach-churning, with powerful overtones of rotting food, urine, excrement and body odour. Disease is rife and tuberculosis, typhoid and cholera are alarmingly common complaints. In October 1995, Justice Emmanuel O'kubasu stated that prisons in Kenya were 'death chambers'.

The same month, Home Affairs Minister Francis Lotodo reported that 814 prisoners had died in jails during the first nine months of that year, mainly from dysentery and diarrohea.

The twin horrors of rape and HIV/Aids continually rear up. One prisoner suggested that scantily clad bodies in close proximity to one another were bound to encourage sexual activity.

In 2003 there were 3,800 prisoners within the walls of Nairobi's jail when it was built to contain just 800

Corporal punishment is permitted, with adults subject to a maximum of 12 strokes of a hippo-hide whip. Mostly, prisoners are beaten for failing to obey orders. Other punishments include a restricted diet and solitary confinement. Although some 400 prisoners at the Nairobi prison are on death row there have been no hangings for 20 years.

Beyond the whippings, though, lies a shockingly brutal culture that has spread among enforcers in and around Kenyan jails.

In September 2000, six death row prisoners were killed at the maximum security King'ong'o prison. The Prison Department alleged that they had tried to escape and had died falling from the high perimeter walls. The police said they had been shot dead as they tried to escape.

However, medical examinations shortly after their deaths found no evidence of gunshot injuries, but discovered that their eyes had been gouged out. Post-mortems further revealed that their skulls had been crushed with a blunt object, and that several of the corpses had fractured limbs. Two other

Dr Veronique Vasseur, head doctor at La Santé prison, who wrote an exposé of conditions there

If I said nothing I would be an accomplice to all this, and that I cannot tolerate - Dr Veronique Vasseur

inmates also attempted to escape with the six. One was injured during the break out, subsequently arrested and severely beaten by police during interrogation. The other managed to escape but was shot dead by police during a raid on a town bar.

But poor conditions and brutality are not confined only to cash-starved prisons in the third world.

FRANCE

DOCTOR'S NOTES

An appalling environment at the Paris jail, La Santé, was revealed when Dr Veronique Vasseur published an extraordinary exposé in 2000. Despite the medieval horrors contained in the pages of the book, few doubted that her

words were an accurate reflection of what went on inside the jail's grey walls. She had, after all, been the prison doctor there for seven years.

The prison was built in the 1860s and can accommodate 1,200 prisoners, although the roll is often far greater than that.

Prisoners became so desperate at La Santé, she said, that they swallowed rat poison, forks or drain cleaner to escape the sordid conditions.

Skin diseases were rampant because showers were only available twice a week, although temperatures sometimes soared to more than 100 degrees Fahrenheit in cramped cells holding four prisoners.

Vasseur was horrified to discover evidence of bread scabies, a disease caused by mouldy loaves unknown in France except during times of extreme deprivation, like the Second World War.

About a third of inmates at La Santé were addicted to something while between five and ten per cent were HIV positive.

Cells were crawling with vermin. Inmates crammed their clothes in the cracks in the walls of their cells to keep the rats out, while most of the mattresses were alive with lice and other insects. Sometimes prisoners captured them in glass jars as evidence or sport. During a press visit hastily arranged after the book's launch, a mouse was seen sauntering down a corridor, untroubled by the presence of journalists and prison staff.

Sexual assault was commonplace. Some of the weaker prisoners, Dr. Vasseur discovered, had been turned into slaves by their cellmates.

She saw one man being pinned down by eight guards as they tried to administer an injection. When he lashed out he was dispatched to a single cell in the punishment block where she found him 15 days later suffering from chronic dehydration. The guards, she discovered, had cut the water supply to the cell. Beatings by guards were frequently meted out, she insisted.

'You cannot work and see the things I saw and not speak out,' said Dr. Vasseur. 'If I said nothing I would be an accomplice to all this, and that I cannot tolerate.'

She had some backing from the Council of Europe which, following an investigation, branded French jails as 'repulsively dirty'.

A curious quirk in the French legal system means that many prisoners held in jail have not been convicted of any crime. They are kept there while investigations into the case are carried out. These last on average for four months. As the 21st century dawned there were 57,844 people in French prisons, of whom 20,143 were on remand. Indeed, a considerable number will be released without any formal charges. Yet they will have been subjected to the same grim conditions as convicted criminals.

Soon after Vasseur's book appeared some of France's high-profile former prisoners signed a petition deploring prison conditions all over France. These included, they claimed, acrid cells, systematic rape, humiliation of visiting families, primitive health care, drug dealing by guards and the corruption of young people habitually housed with seasoned criminals.

A former mayor who signed the petition, Jean-Michel Boucheron, said that when he was jailed for corruption, his cell at La Santé was just above the punishment blocks. 'My eyes stung regularly from the tear gas thrown into isolation cells by guards,' he said. In another prison, he claims he had to 'paddle' through blood 'left by a prisoner who committed suicide after banging on his cell door all night without getting help.'

The claims might go some way to explain why 118 prisoners committed suicide in France in 2000 and more than 1,000 made an attempt to end their lives. There were 1,362 cases of self-mutilation, 953 hunger strikes lasting longer than seven days and 278 attacks by inmates on guards.

The book also sparked two government commissions of inquiry. Justice Minister Elisabeth Guigou admitted that France's prison system was facing difficulties. 'The situation in a lot of our prisons is not worthy of a country such as ours,' she said. Two years later little had been done to remedy the problems although the commissions had called for urgent action. One observer maintained that the inside of French jails was still 'a descent into hell'.

NORTH KOREA

MODERN CONCENTRATION CAMPS

In North Korea concentration camps, along with regular jails, are used to contain 'wrongdoers' and their entire families.

North Korea has a secretive Stalinist regime led by Kim Jong-Il, son of state founder Kim Il-Sung. Its aim is to control the thoughts as well as the actions of the population and this is where concentration camps come in. Their purpose is to re-educate everyone who has revealed individual or critical thought so that the 'students' revert to unquestioning obedience to the state. Families are included in case relatives of the 'rebel' have been infected by rogue notions.

Like jails, concentration camps provide a cheap labour force and so they frequently become centres of industry vital to the survival of the regime. North Korea is one of the world's poorest nations and the camp workers are hard driven by quotas. Yet the emphasis is also on the humiliation and annihilation of those imprisoned behind razor wire fences and under the eagle eye of armed guards.

Yodok is just such a place, lying high in the Korean mountains and largely hidden from public view. There are several groups of huts called 'villages'. Detainees labour in the fields,

Prisoners of North Korea's concentration camp regime erect barbed wire around a compound

in gold mines, chop down trees or work in clothes factories. Discipline is tough, and detainees are executed if they try to flee. Adults are subjected to hard labour all day, every day, while children are under the cosh for half a day.

Food is in short supply all over North Korea as state policies have ruined national harvests. At Kodok, prisoners receive a ration of only 300 grams of maize a day and some supplement their diets with nightmarish food-stuffs such as rats, mice, frogs and frogspawn.

Chul-Hwan Kang was taken to Yodok concentration camp with his family at the age of nine and held for ten years. 'Few people at Yodok survived more than ten years. I had a strong will to survive. There was nothing I did not eat: snakes, rats, frogs, whatever I could lay my hands on. Some of us would find

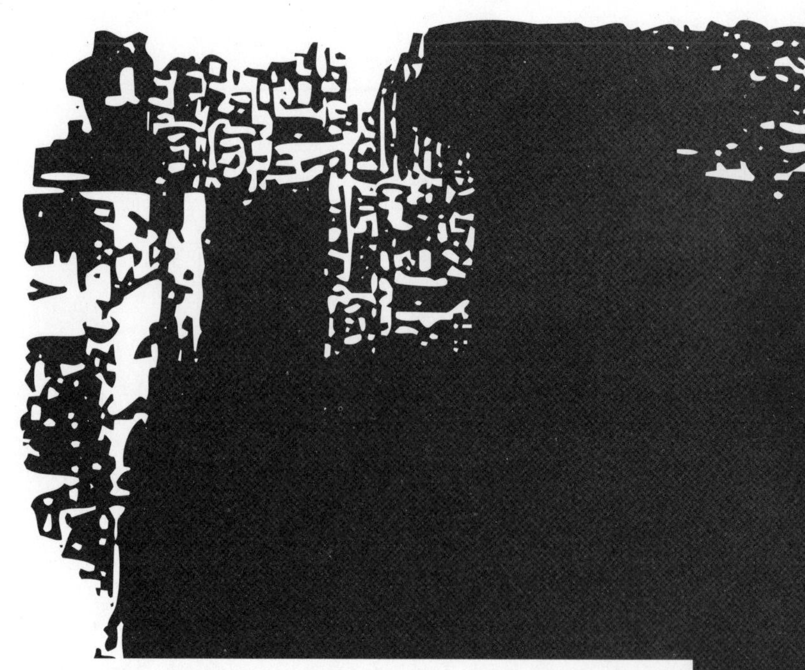

'I witnessed the execution of five prisoners who had tried to escape. The men were bound and masked, made to kneel down and each shot with three bullets.'

worms in the ground or from the river. Some could not do this. Those who could not eat anything just perished.'

From the moment he arrived as a child, Kang was given a quota and put to work. Inexperienced, he had to work through the night to collect the required amount of fire-wood. Children were also put to work sifting gold bits from sand in the river, planting corn, mining limestone, and, when they were older, logging:

> 'When we worked to cut down trees, we were told by the guards, "look you have to be careful, this is for export to Japan." We had ropes around the trees to make sure that they fell softly and weren't broken. The guards told us the logs could not be exported to Japan if they were broken.
>
> 'So many people were killed and crippled handling these trees. [People often] fell off the

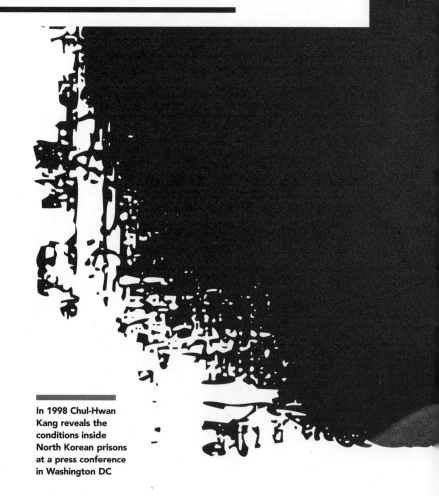

In 1998 Chul-Hwan Kang reveals the conditions inside North Korean prisons at a press conference in Washington DC

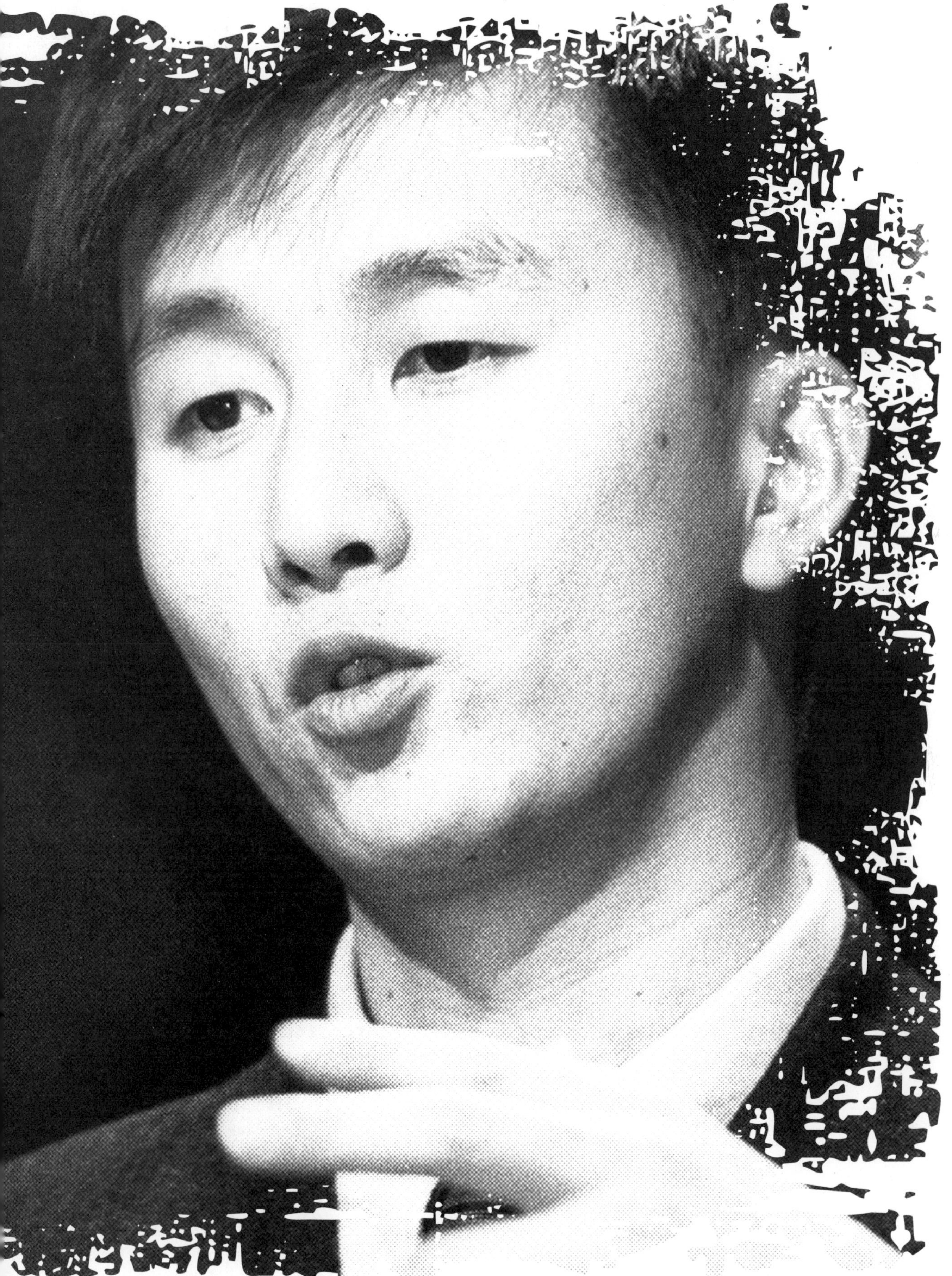

Eun-Cheol Kim was dispatched to Yodok, North Korea, on a treason charge when he was 19 and put to work in construction. Like other workers, he laboured day and night in summer and winter:

"I had to wake up at 4:30 in the morning, support the agricultural work unit, carry the fertilizers, plough, and return to the camp at 7:00 for breakfast. Basic construction work started at 7:30 in the morning, when I had to dig the ground, mix cement with my hands, build the security office, and later expand it.

'While I was in the construction work unit for the three years, I built various facilities for poultry, goats, cows and warehouses . . . which were in fact left empty. Lunch was self-prepared with what was distributed in the morning. We would normally try to pull out grasses or herbs to add to our brass bowls for a more filling feeling in the stomach.

'Normally, we were at work until six or seven in the evening but, blaming the efficiency of our work, they would make us work more, even when it was dark. At night, three teams of six people or two teams of eight would work extra night-time hours. The first team would work from five in the afternoon to one in the morning, the next team from one in the morning to five or six the next day. The last team would work for the rest of the day, meaning that the labor work went on almost 24 hours a day.

'If a person dies in the camp, it is basically another job allocated to the construction work unit to deal with the corpse. When some of us tried to make a coffin for the dead with any sort of wooden panels, we would be pushed to rush, so eventually we just threw the body into the wooden box and nailed them in any manner. We carried the coffins on oxcarts, but once we stumbled on stones, the coffins would break open, throwing the body on to the ground. I would usually be the one to pull the cart, but once the falling body caught my eye, a strong sense of survival would seize me. (It was sad to think that life after death would look like the bodies that fall out of feeble coffins in the camps). The place of burial of these bodies was called the 'grave valley'. The burials usually took place late at night so we would hasten as fast as possible and taking advantage of being in the dark, try to dig whatever was edible and fill our mouths."

trees as they were trimming them. They had to bring the logs down to the foot of the mountain for inspection. If there was any slightest damage, the logs would not pass, then the prisoners would have to do the work all over again. So even on cold winter days we would cover the logs with our clothes to make sure they arrived at the inspection point unharmed. But these were very heavy logs we were carrying; some undernourished prisoners would drop the logs and others would fall down with them, breaking their legs and arms or dying. So many prisoners were killed this way.

Kang recalls how he was kicked unconscious for forgetting to wear his 'good' socks to visit the room containing Kim Il-Sung's picture:

'These were very heavy logs we were carrying; some undernourished prisoners would drop the logs and others would fall down with them, breaking their legs and arms or dying'

'I witnessed the execution of five prisoners who had tried to escape. The men were bound and masked, made to kneel down and each shot with three bullets.'

When he discovered that prisoners were occasionally released for good behaviour on significant dates, he became a model prisoner. In Yodok, detainees have to criticize – and be criticized by – other detainees. Kang Cho Hwan submitted to these sessions of criticizm and self-criticizm twice a week. A session includes extolling the virtues of Kim Jong-Il, listening to comments about articles published in the propagandist Rodong Shinmun newspaper, and learning entire speeches by the 'Great Leader', Kim Jong-Il. He was set free a few days prior to Kim Jong-Il's birthday as part of the camp celebration.

Young Soon Kim recalls some of the reasons why people were sent to Yodok:

'The charges against the inmates at prison camp I5 were the crime of saying that "Kim Il-Sung has a lump on his neck"; breaking the bust of Kim Jung-Il; using a newspaper with Kim Il-Sung's face as wallpaper; watching foreign videos or sharing them with their neighbors; listening to South Korean broadcasts; or, as I did, making a slip of the tongue. People were imprisoned for eight years, I0 years or until death for things that are not considered a crime in a free, democratic society.'

A prison worker at Pusan, North Korea, labours on a construction site

...ON PRISON LIFE

To a warden, Utopia is an escape-proof jail.

— Gregory Nunn (born 1955)

America has the longest prison sentences in the West yet the only condition long sentences demonstrably cure is heterosexuality.

— Bruce Jackson

We who live in prison and in whose lives there is no event but sorrow have to measure time by throbs of pain and the record of bitter moments.

— Oscar Wilde (1854-1900)

The whole value of solitude depends upon one's self; it may be a sanctuary or a prison, a haven of repose or a place of punishment, a heaven or a hell as we ourselves make it.

— John Lubbock (1834-1913)

One of the many lessons that one learns in prison is that things are what they are, will be what they will be.

— Oscar Wilde (1854-1900)

People who claim that sentencing a murderer to 'life without the possibility of parole' protects society just as well as the death penalty ignore three things: 1) life without the possibility of parole does not mean life without the possibility of escape or 2) life without the possibility of killing while in prison or 3) life without the possibility of a liberal governor being elected and issuing a pardon.

— Thomas Sowell, Economist (born 1930)

In jail a man has no personality. He is a minor disposal problem and a few entries on reports. Nobody cares who loves or hates him, what he looks like, what he did with his life. Nobody reacts to him unless he gives trouble. Nobody abuses him. All that is asked of him is that he go quietly to the right cell and remain quiet when he gets there. There is nothing to fight against, nothing to be mad at. The jailers are quiet men without animosity or sadism. All this stuff you read about men yelling and screaming, beating against the bars, running spoons along them, guards rushing in with clubs – all that is for the big house. A good jail is one of the quietest places in the world. Life in jail is in suspension.

— Raymond Chandler (1888–1959)

To assert in any case that a man must be absolutely cut off from society because he is absolutely evil amounts to saying that society is absolutely good, and no-one in his right mind will believe this today.

— Albert Camus (1913–1960)

2 GANGSTER RAP

A RELATIVELY new phenomenon, prison gangs have quickly established power bases in major jails around the world. Typically, gangs are run by ruthless and violent megalomaniacs. Campaigns by the authorities to unseat the kingpins have been singularly unsuccessful.

In the beginning prisoners gathered under the gang umbrella to shield themselves from the brutality meted out by others in the system. The reason behind their unity was understandable, even noble.

Inevitably, however, the gangs and their members were contaminated by vices like greed and egotism, and became fuelled by drug money. Thanks to the culture of terror they generate, the existence of gangs affects prisoners, their families and even prison guards. And the ominous power of gangs is no longer caged inside penitentiaries. The slickest are as potent on city streets as they are behind bars.

A municipal bus goes up in flames in Sao Paulo, Brazil, in July 2006. This was just one attack on government property organized that month by the First Capital Command prison gang

BRAZIL

With a population of some 11 million, Sao Paulo is the biggest city in the Southern Hemisphere. It stands proud with its skyscrapers, its bustling business community and its vibrant culture that captivates residents and visitors alike.

Yet for four days in May 2006 the place was paralysed after street warfare that left 170 people dead and 93 more wounded. More than 60 buses were burned. Government buildings were firebombed, roads were impassable and residents stayed at home. All 70 state penitentiaries were hit by riots.

The carnage and destruction was breath taking. But perhaps the most eye-opening

aspect of the bloody episode was that it began on the orders of a prison gang boss, given from inside his cell by mobile phone. It was his response to a government plan to mute prison gang power. Ironically, perhaps, in a city with the motto 'I am not led, I lead', 'Marcola' Comacho was making a direct challenge as to who really ruled the city.

Secret plans

The government's idea was simple and strategic: significant players from the prison gang First Capital Command, better known by its Portuguese initials PCC (Primeiro Comando da Capital),would be removed from Sao Paulo's prisons to jails in remote areas in order to take them out of the communications loop.

It was unveiled at a secret meeting and surprise was to be a key element of its success. However, the architects of the ploy didn't reckon on the long tentacles of the gang. Its hierarchy knew about the plans almost instantly when a government employee divulged the meeting's secrets to a PCC lawyer. In the mayhem that followed prison guards were killed at their homes and off-duty police officers were gunned down as they relaxed in bars.

The *Folha de Sao Paulo* newspaper reported receiving a video – supposedly produced by the PCC – featuring a masked man flanked by machine guns and sticks of dynamite. In the video, he reportedly made demands in the name of the 'party', saying at one point: 'Don't mess with our families and we won't mess with yours.' Threats of violence also circulated via the internet.

The gang's ominously precise organization chilled the hearts of the city's residents, who found themselves faced with the reality of daily battles between trigger-happy policemen and vicious gunmen, although some remained convinced that the gang was merely the scapegoat of an incompetent government.

'They link this to the PCC because the government doesn't want to take responsibility for controlling delinquency,' said Bezerra da Silva, standing next to a wooden stool that he keeps padlocked to a streetlight. 'They blame the PCC, saying it's a huge problem they can't control, and they wash their hands of everything.'

Violent history

Terrible though events in Sao Paulo were that month, the episode was just one in a series linked to the PCC that shocked the world. In December there were 12 orchestrated attacks

❑ **Journalist J. J. Maloney talks about the fear that fellow inmates can inspire behind bars:**

"I'm talking about a gnawing kind of anxiety that puts a sharp edge on all your senses. It permeates your subconscious. It catapults survival to the top of your list of priorties.

Wanting to survive in prison can make an actor out of you. There are certain roles you can play that enhance your chances of being accepted by other convicts, of being left alone, respected; and respect, ultimately, is the key to 'making it' in prison.

'When I was sent to the Missouri State Penitentiary at Jefferson City, in February 1960, there were 2,500 men inside 'the walls'. The white convicts slept three to a cell (except for several hundred in the one-man cells). The blacks slept as many as eight to a cell.

'Stabbings and killings, robberies and rapes were common. Dope was easier to get in prison than it was on the streets. There were men in prison who were said to make more money each year from dope and gambling than the warden was paid. There were captains on the guard force who owed their souls to certain convicts.

'You never knew whom you might have trouble with. The reasons for murder and mayhem made little sense to anyone except the convicts. So hundreds of men either carried a knife or had one they could get to in an emergency."

in just four hours on buses and police targets, which left 19 dead and 20 injured. Again the go ahead was given from inside prison.

In June 2005, a PCC riot at Presidente Venceslau Penitentiary, 373 miles west of Sao Paulo, ended in the death of five prisoners, whose decapitated heads were paraded on long poles atop the prison roof. It is thought that the victims were former members of the PCC who were being kept in isolation for their own protection when the riot broke out. Rioters told local reporters that they erupted into violence because they had suffered 'humiliations and repression'.

Judge Machado Dias was assassinated by the PCC in 2003 after dispatching high-profile members to a maximum-security prison.

In February 2001 more than 8,000 prison guards and visitors, including 1,700 children, were taken hostage when trouble flared at 18 prisons in and around Sao Paulo. Eight people - both prisoners and prison staff - died before peace was restored.

Violence in Brazilian jails has shocked even experienced observers. 'What is peculiar to Brazil is the exceptional level and type of violence,' Andy Barclay, project director of the International Centre for Prison Studies, said. 'There are, of course, killings in other systems around the world but I've never come across elsewhere the torture and decapitation like you find in Brazil.'

The courtyard of the Carandiru prison in Sao Paulo, Brazil, since demolished

However, the PCC initially had sound reasons for its formation. It was founded in Taubate Prison in 1993 from the ranks of the prison soccer team as a response to the massacre of prisoners at Latin America's biggest penitentiary, the notorious Carandiru Prison in the suburbs of Sao Paulo in 1992. When the killing stopped 111 inmates lay dead.

The shocking incident had unremarkable beginnings. A fight between two inmates – nicknamed 'Barba' and 'Coelho' – had been broken up by prison staff who subsequently locked down the cellblock.

That might have been the end of the trouble

were it not for chronic overcrowding. Carandiru , built to hold some 3,000 prisoners, was packed with a population of at least 7,000. Prisoners, compelled to sleep in shifts because there were too few beds, were vulnerable to diseases like scabies and tuberculosis, which only contributed to the tinderbox atmosphere. Within a few hours the prisoners had control of the area. Observers insist, however, that no hostages had been taken and there had been no attempt to escape.

The authorities lined up Sao Paulo's military police to regain control of the prison. Inmates apparently tossed weapons out the prison windows and hung lengths of material down the outside walls to denote a truce.

Yet police officers armed with machine guns, automatic pistols and assault rifles rampaged through the floors and the corridors, mowing down prisoners as they dived for cover.

Police officers armed with machine guns, automatic pistols and assault rifles rampaged through the corridors.

An official report discovered that 515 shots were fired, killing 103 prisoners. Eight died of other wounds, possibly administered by fellow inmates. No policemen was killed. Forensic reports proved that the shots were fired into rather than out of the cells, casting doubt on police claims that they acted in self defence. The majority of bullet wounds were to the heads and chests of the dead, suggesting a 'shoot to kill' policy.

It all unfolded on the eve of municipal elections, during which law and order had been a key issue. An investigation into the episode took years to complete, by which time the PCC was in full swing. Eventually, it seemed that justice would be done.

'Reprisal' killings

In 2001 Colonel Ubiratan Guimaraes, who had commanded the police during the trouble, was sentenced to 632 years in jail for sending in the riot police to quell the disturbance. However, the sentence was overturned on a technicality the following year.

When the body of 63-year-old Guimaraes was found in 2006 having bled to death after being shot in the stomach it was thought a vengeful PCC might have been responsible. Carandiru chief prison warden, Jose Ismael Pedrosa, who was also implicated in prisoner deaths, was likewise killed in suspicious circumstances in 2005 amid rumours of PCC involvement.

The government acknowledged mistakes made at Carandiru and the prison was demolished in 2002. However, it was already too late to stem the potency of the gang that was equally fired up by the squalid conditions in other overcrowded jails.

Today the PCC has an estimated 125,000 members, making it the largest gang in the Western world. To be inducted into the PCC means 'blooding a finger', that is swearing to observe a 16-point constitution that includes kidnapping officials. The ceremony involves cutting a finger to produce blood. That is why prison guards have been taken hostage by the hundreds since its inception. Without any sense of satire, its slogan is 'Liberty, Justice and Peace'.

It has won significant victories against the authorities, including the provision of better food, increased visiting rights and, allegedly, extra television sets in prisons during the football World Cup.

With prisoners deprived of the bare necessities, the gang has strengthened its core support by providing essential items that include toothbrushes, soap and food. It also has a network of 'brothers' and 'sisters', prisoners who support the gang but who are not themselves members. But if it began with fraternal and gallant intentions it has now moved into the murky realms of organized crime. Efforts to improve prison conditions have subsequently been sidelined.

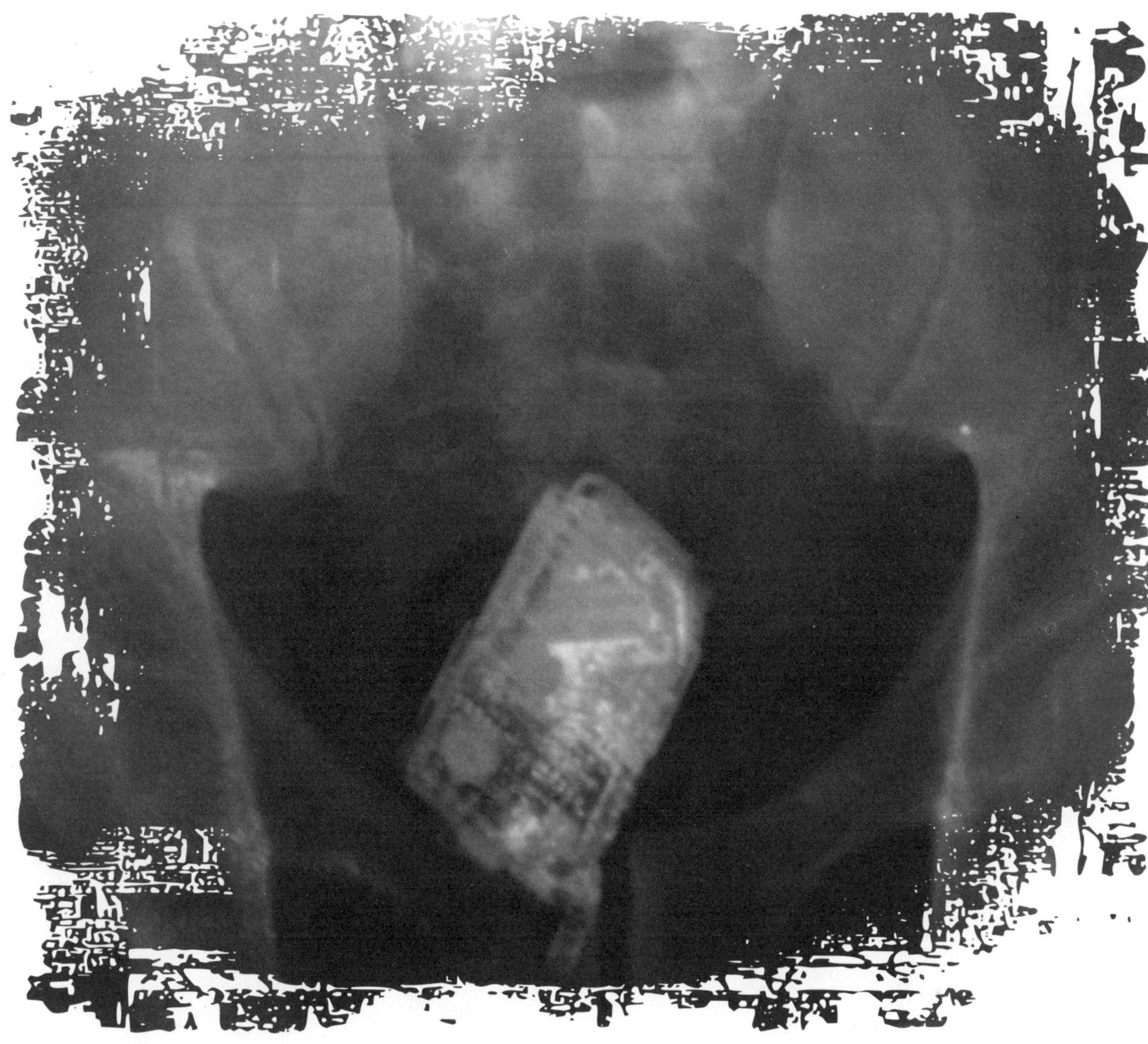

An X-ray taken at a prison in San Salvador reveals a mobile phone in the intestines of an inmate

Appalling conditions

Five years after the PCC began, conditions in Brazilian prisons were still sufficiently poor to attract the condemnation of the human rights group Amnesty International. In a 1998 report it gives some insight into why the gang has hit such a rich vein of support. 'Weekly riots and almost daily serious assaults indicate that in many prisons the authorities have lost control. Corruption is rife. Staff entrusted with the care and rehabilitation of prisoners do not have the resources to carry out their jobs. Doctors who fail to turn up for work are not disciplined, and there are simply too few legal aid lawyers to guarantee prisoners an adequate defense. Prison guards do not receive professional training in important skills such as restraint methods, and themselves risk violence and illness. Despite the enormous responsibilities of their work, they have no official guidelines to direct them and are not effectively monitored. If they beat, torture or kill a prisoner, there are no effective complaint mechanisms in place to hold them accountable for their actions. Very few investigations result in a criminal prosecution.'

Cell phones

In the 21st century the gang has continually improved its profile. One of the key tools of its organization is the mobile phone, smuggled in to every prison and cloned so that tracing it is impossible. It is vital for co-ordinating attacks on both sides of prison walls. Since 2002, when Marcola, or 'Playboy', Camacho took control of the PCC, the expertise of the Colombian gangs has been sought, as well as guns, from counterparts in Paraguay. Camacho is serving

a 44-year sentence for bank robbery. According to the Brazilian news source Epoca, he is a dapper intellectual. During a recent search of his cell several political manifestos were found, alongside Sun Tzu's *The Art of War*, Machiavelli's *The Prince* and biographies of Che Guevara. Following media coverage of the May 2006 fighting he was featured on the front cover of several magazines in Brazil, enhancing his iconic status among prisoners.

The PCC members who are responsible for communications are known as pilots while those in charge of prison discipline are referred to as 'Bin Ladens'. As a result of its expanding influence, instances of violence between inmates have plummeted as no one dares to scrap without PCC say-so.

The PCC has struck an agreement with its counterpart in Rio de Janeiro, the Red Command. Such efficient blanket coverage means there's little opportunity for rival gangs to get off the ground. Hostage taking continues to be one of its favourite tools.

One unnamed prison officer told a newspaper that he was in no doubt about who called the shots in Brazilian prisons. 'Everyone in the prison is a hostage of the PCC. They make all the decisions, not the prison administrators.'

His words were echoed by BBC reporter Tom Gibb who says the PCC and its associated gangs possess enormous power within Brazil's prison system.

'A lot of the prisoners are very frightened of it,' he said. 'A lot of the prisoners who are not involved may themselves in many ways be hostages.'

Heidi Cerneka, who works for the Catholic prison ministry in Sao Paulo, concurred with this troubling theory. 'The State, according to many prison employees that we know and even some directors, no longer controls the prisons. The PCC does. Prison directors have been known to make implicit or explicit agreements with the leaders of the PCC. Directors agree that they'll let them do whatever they want on the inside, as long as no riots occur in that particular prison.

'Unfortunately, the best place to buy drugs in the state of Sao Paulo is inside the prisons. One can purchase alcohol, drugs, arms and cell phones in the prisons if one has enough money or connections. According to inmates, most of these products enter the prison in the hands of corrupt and greedy guards.

'According to the prison system, most of it enters through family members on visiting day. However, family members are literally strip searched before entering. Recently, a machine gun was confiscated at the end of a rebellion. It is hard to imagine a family member managing to sneak in a machine gun without the assistance of some guard somewhere.'

With the Brazilian prison population trebling between 1992 and 2004, the government unwittingly supplies numerous new recruits on a regular basis.

USA

THE GANGS OF AMERICA

Of course, prison gangs are common to all countries and continents. It was during the 1990s that this new threat to prison stability in the US was identified, as behind bars disturbances leapt by 400 per cent. For the first time the muscle wielded by prison gangs was understood by prison authorities.

From their cell, albeit without the advantage of cell phones, US gang leaders could control extortion, drug dealing, prostitution and even order murder to take place. Gangs and gang membership have been mushrooming in recent years and prison authorities have been fighting a rearguard action to contain prison gang power.

One survey has put prison gang membership in the US at more than 300,000. In Illinois it is estimated that 60 per cent of the prison population is affiliated to a gang.

Renowned for their slick organization, the gangs orchestrate the supply of drugs in prisons. In America gangs generally divide along racial lines and their existence, at least in the beginning, had an almost meritorious rationale – they claimed to stand for the defence of vulnerable minorities behind bars.

The biggest and most threatening gangs – known to the authorities as Security Threat Groups or STGs – have been identified as follows over the page:

Riot police stand guard over inmates at the Belem Prison in Sao Paulo, Brazil, after quelling a riot

A member of the Aryan Brotherhood displays his gang tattoo in a California state prison

Aryan Brotherhood

A white supremacist gang, the Aryan Brotherhood, also known as the Brand, has been in existence since the 1960s, evolving out of a white, Irish-influenced gang known as the Blue Birds. It devised an oath of allegiance to bind its members together, which still holds good today.

'I will stand by my brother.
My brother will come before all others.
My life is forfeit should I fail my brother.
I will honour my brother in peace as in war.'

Although it still indulges in Nazi insignia it is better known by the symbols of the shamrock, the initials AB and three sixes; and it is these that feature in tattoos denoting gang membership. Wannabes who display such tattoos before being accepted into the Brotherhood are likely to have it burned off – they might even be killed. Like other white supremacist groups, it cherishes the number 18, which denotes the first and eighth letters of the alphabet, the initials of Adolf Hitler.

The Brotherhood functions best in an atmosphere of fear and loathing. A peerless reputation for ruthlessness is rooted in numerous killings and it's said that in 1969 Charles Manson, the convicted serial killer and race-hate preacher, was not sufficiently violent to join its ranks. A blip in AB power was reported to the director of the Federal Bureau of Investigation (FBI) in 1982 following an interview with an informer.

'The AB was organized in the California state prison system but within the last several years they have become an influence within the federal penal system and their activities tend to be uncontrolled.

'Things are not currently going well within the AB as many members have become users of drugs, act in a petty manner and do not live by their lifelong sworn code of conduct.'

Mourners give the Black Panther salute at the funeral of gang member George Jackson on 21 August 1971. Jackson had been killed attempting to escape from San Quentin prison

Nonetheless it has survived and thrived. Like other prison gangs, its primary business these days is trading drugs, extortion, racketeering and prostitution. Members released from prison are expected to do their utmost to support those still incarcerated. In 2002 an indictment against 40 alleged AB members and associates revealed the long arm of the gang.

'The Aryan Brotherhood enforces its rules and promotes discipline among its members and associates by murdering, attempting to murder, conspiring to murder, assaulting and threatening those who violate the enterprise's rules or pose a threat to the enterprise . . . Inmates and others who do not follow the orders of the Aryan Brotherhood risk being murdered, as is anyone who uses violence against an Aryan Brotherhood member. Inmates who co-operate with law enforcement authorities are also subject to being murdered.'

David Grann, a gang investigator, told The *New Yorker* magazine: 'The gang selects only

the most violent and capable individuals to become "made" members - individuals who are, as one former gang member put it, "master manipulators." But I also think that the leaders have been able to operate for decades because so many of their crimes are done in the cloistered world of prison, where the public doesn't see them and where many of their victims are hardened cons.'

He believes prisons and gangs like the AB bring out the worst in people. 'I do think that there are instances where individuals come in as bank robbers or drug dealers and, after being socialized in the violent, apartheid world of prisons and the gangs there, are transformed into conscienceless killers.'

Black Guerrilla Family

At first the agenda of the Black Guerrilla Family (BGF) was archly political. It was formed in 1966 inside San Quentin Prison by former Black Panther member George Jackson with the aim of eradicating racism, maintaining dignity in prison and overthrowing the US government.

Among its members were men from the Black Family, the Black Vanguard, the Black Liberation Army, the Symbionese Liberation Army and the Weathermen Underground, all demonstrably capable of extreme violence.

Chicago-born Jackson was still a teenager when he was thrown in jail following a $70 gas station hold up. He would never be a free man again. In 1970, along with two others, he was charged with murdering a guard at California's Soledad Prison. The slaying was carried out in retaliation for the killing of three black activists by a prison guard, who was later acquitted of murder charges. Afterwards Jackson became known as one of the Soledad Brothers and, while in solitary confinement for 23 hours a day, devoted himself to reading and writing. His two works, *Blood in My Eye* and *Soledad Brother*, which expounded his Marxist ideology, were widely acclaimed.

Also in 1970, Jackson's 17-year-old brother Jonathan burst into a Marin County courtroom aiming to free a trio of San Quentin prisoners. At the same time he took Judge Harold Haley hostage, demanding Jackson's liberation in exchange for Haley's life.

However, police opened fire on the getaway car, killing Jackson and two of the prisoners. It's likely a gun carried inside the vehicle killed Haley. The prisoner who survived the shoot out was given a life sentence for his involvement.

As it happened, George Jackson did not live much beyond his brother. He was gunned down in the prisoner yard at San Quentin in 1971, where he had been transferred prior to his trial. Prison authorities insisted that Jackson had been armed and was instrumental in a prison

riot that day that claimed the lives of three guards and two prisoners – charges denied by his fellow prisoners. Opinion remains sharply divided about Jackson.

Stanley Williams, a founder of the Crips gang, dedicated his 1998 book *Life in Prison*, in part, to George Jackson. It did him no favours. In his response to Williams' appeal for clemency, Governor Arnold Schwarzenegger claimed that this dedication was 'a significant indicator that Williams is not reformed and that he still sees violence and lawlessness as a legitimate means to address societal problems.'

With Jackson dead the highbrow aims of the group dissipated. The BGF became as immersed in drug trafficking, prostitution and racketeering as other prison gangs.

Recently it has formed alliances with street gangs including the Crips, the Bloods and the up and coming Gangster Disciples to maintain its stranglehold on narcotics transactions in certain areas. It has adopted a new profile or identity known as New Man/New Woman or New Afrika Revolutionary Nation. However, the tattoo of a dragon encircling a prison tower with a guard at its mercy, crossed weapons and the letters BGF still stand.

Right: Raol Leon of the Mexican Mafia in his cell at California's Pelican Bay prison

Mexican Mafia

The roots of the Mexican Mafia lay in the 1950s when a group of 13 Mexican inmates at the Deuel Vocational Institute, a correctional facility in California, formed a gang to protect one another from antagonistic inmates. When prison authorities tried to break up the gang by sending members to other prisons they only succeeded in boosting its membership as each gang member turned recruiter. When members were released from prison and returned to the streets the gang went from strength to brutal strength.

It's also known as La Eme and members used to be distinguishable by red bandannas or T-shirts.

Another identity of the Mexican Mafia is the Surenos, which strictly speaking applies only to those from Southern California.

As if to underline its success, the La Eme even sold protection to imprisoned godfathers of the Italian Mafia. One of the gang's architects, Joe 'Peg Leg' Morgan, was a white man who adopted Hispanic culture and in the past there have been blacks and Caucasians in its ranks. However, at the moment the gang's hierarchy has given the green light for ethnic

Far Left: Young members of the Crips Gang display their weapons at Compton, Los Angeles

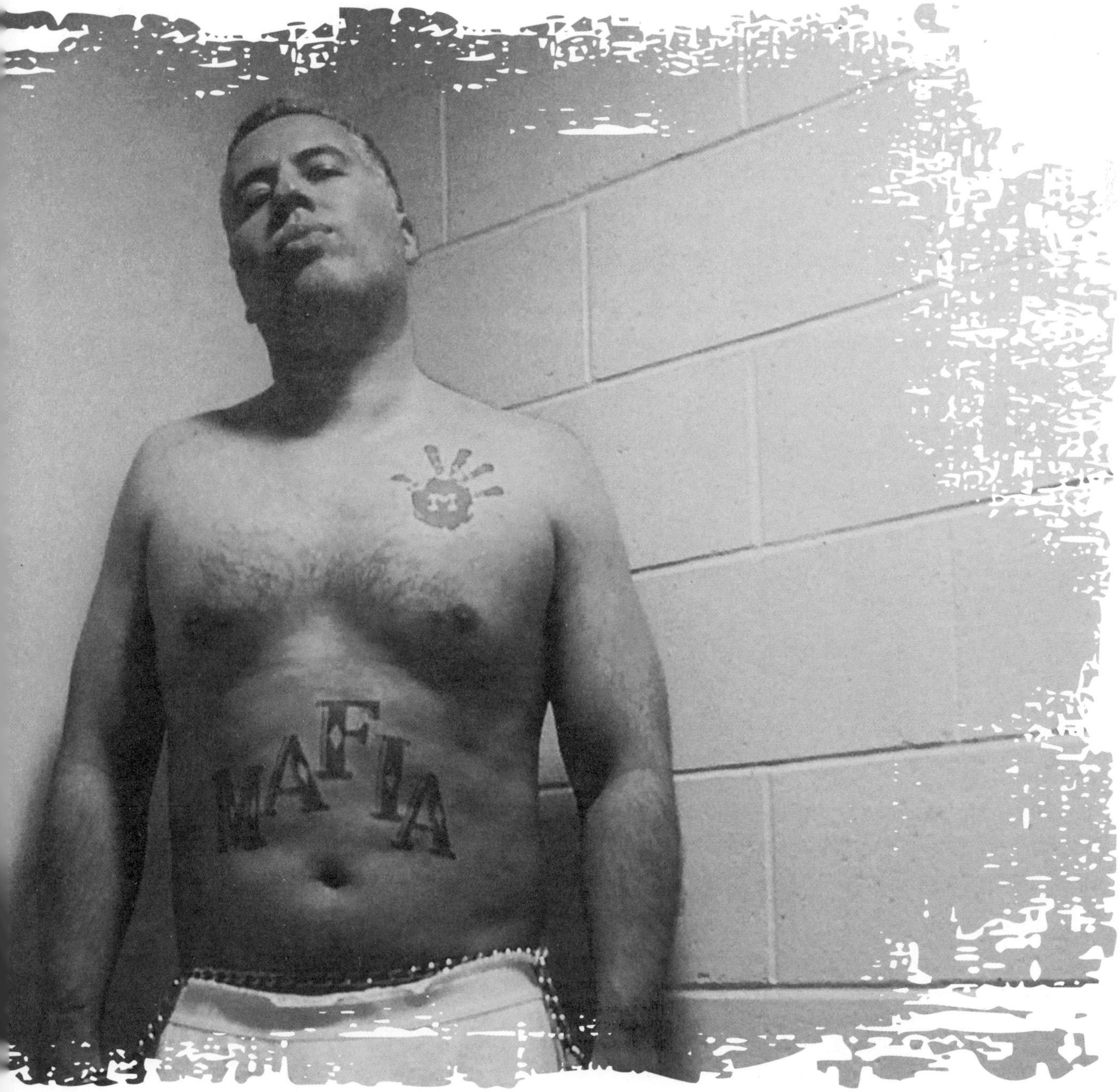

cleansing in its strongholds on the streets, meaning that any gang member who sees a black man should kill him.

After a prison bust up at San Quentin in 1968 over the theft of a pair of shoes the Mexican Mafia and La Nuestra Familia (NF) – the prominent and adverserial Latino gang – became sworn enemies. The owner of the shoes was Hector Padilla, a member of La Nuestra Familia who shared a cell with Robert 'Robot' Salas of the Mexican Mafia. Carlos 'Pieface' Ortega, one of Salas's comrades, apparently stole the shoes and Padilla was killed in the fight that ensued.

One of the gang's early leaders, Rudy 'Cheyenne' Cadena, encouraged recently released members to take part in laudable community work like drug rehabilitation programmes. By doing so they gained access to millions of dollars in government grant money, the proceeds of which they passed on to the Mexican Mafia. This lead to a wave of corruption scandals in California that exposed the deep involvement of the Mexican Mafia in public life.

A visionary who believed criminal gangs could unite to challenge the US government, Cadena organized a truce with the Black Guerrilla Family in 1970 and the following year urged Latino gangs to unite.

It was with this ambition in mind that he arranged to meet the leaders of La Nuestra Familia in a second-floor prison cell at Palm Hall, in the Chino Institute for men on 17 December 1972. The NF response was swift and uncompromising. Two members of the NF repeatedly stabbed Cadena. When his stricken body was tossed over the guard rail another NF member weighed in. Cadena died from more than 50 stab wounds.

Cadena was among 36 inmates to be murdered that year in California – but only one of six whose assailants were not thought to be from the Mexican Mafia.

The practice of milking federal programmes continued. In 1976 paroled gang member Michael Delia launched Project Get Going, ostensibly to assist drug users, with $228,000 of government money. He accessed the cash through the talents of his wife, Ellen, who was adept at grant applications.

Within a year Ellen was shot dead in Sacramento, apparently on her way to tell the authorities about gang involvement in the project. Her husband ordered the hit.

Eighteen days earlier the same gunmen assassinated Gilbert Roybal after he announced he was leaving the gang. The extraordinary ability of the gang's top brass to look after business from within a prison cell has continued. In 1990 Joe Arriaga was murdered, presumably as punishment for owing $30,000 in taxes to the Mexican Mafia, which takes 10 per cent of every drug transaction carried out in the areas it runs.

Activities were further expanded in 1984 when a Texas branch of the Mexican Mafia was started. Organized by Herbie Huerta after he brokered an agreement with the existing California mafia, it is known as Mexikanemi or La Emi.

According to analyst Robert Fong (1990), the Texas Mafia's Constitution outlines 12 principal rules:

- Membership is for life.
- Every member must be prepared to sacrifice his life or take another's life at any time when required.
- Every member shall strive to overcome his weakness to achieve discipline within the Mexikanemi brotherhood.
- Never let the Mexikanemi down.
- The sponsoring member is totally responsible for the behavior of the new recruit. If the new recruit turns out to be a

Within a year Ellen was shot dead in Sacramento, apparently on her way to tell the authorities about gang involvement in the project. Her husband ordered the hit.

traitor, it is the sponsoring member's responsibility to eliminate the recruit.

- ❑ When disrespected by a stranger or a group, all members of the Mexikanemi will unite to destroy the person or the other group completely.
- ❑ Always maintain a high level of integrity.
- ❑ Never release the Mexikanemi business to others.
- ❑ Every member has the right to express opinions, ideas, contradictions and constructive criticisms.
- ❑ Every member has the right to organize, educate, arm, and defend the Mexikanemi.
- ❑ Every member has the right to wear the tattoo of the Mexikanemi symbol.
- ❑ The Mexikanemi is a criminal organization and therefore will participate in all aspects of criminal interest for monetary benefits.

In 1992 a film called *American Me*, directed by and starring actor Edward James Olmos, focused on the formation of the Eme. Part of it was shot at Folsom Prison and featured real inmates in small roles. However, the hierarchy of the Eme was far from pleased with the movie, believing it 'disrespected' one of the gang founders, Rudy 'Cheyenne' Cadena. Two people who worked as consultants on the film – Charles 'Charlie Brown' Manriquez and Ana Lizarraga – were shot dead in an apparent reprisal, although observers point out that both could have crossed the Eme in a variety of ways, not just through their connection with the film. Police learned from a gang snitch that the killing of Olmos had also been mooted. At the time the actor, best known for his role in *Miami Vice*, was reportedly paying extortion money to the Eme and had sought extra protection from the Los Angeles Police Department.

La Nuestra Familia

A potent prison force, La Nuestra Familia was created as a response to the Mexican Mafia by rural Hispanics in Northern California known as Nortenos. They took exception to the muscle flexing of the urban gang members in the south of the state – the border between north and south lies at Fresno and Bakersfield – and banded together to better retaliate. Its tattoo usually incorporates a bloodied dagger and its favoured colour is blue.

The NF is paramilitary in organization with a Supreme Commander, generals, captains and lieutenants in charge of its soldiers. Recruits are schooled in weapons making, sports, Mexican-American history, and boot camp-like chants, which are used at night to intimidate other inmates as they try to sleep. This is done to prepare aspirants for 21 questions they must successfully answer before they can be admitted into the NF.

Affiliation to the NF is for life. Its long and detailed manifesto includes the provision: 'A familiano will remain a familiano member until death or otherwise discharged from the organization. He will always be subject to put the interests of the organization first and always above everything else, in prison or out.'

It was, in part, the automatic death sentence invoked against NF members perceived to be traitors, cowards or deserters – costing hundreds of lives – that prompted a massive law enforcement operation against it beginning in 1998. Operation Black Widow, which cost $5 million, was also an attempt to mop up the massive amount of drug activity in gang strongholds. Detectives benefited from high-level informants and one man helped secure taped and video evidence. Despite accusations that law enforcement officers stood by while gang assassinations were carried out, 13 defendants – including six from the secure unit at Pelican Bay Prison – were eventually found guilty of scores of crimes. However, the police were not convinced that the gang had been shut down, even temporarily.

'[This is] at best, the cutting off of the head of a poisonous snake – knowing that as we speak it is already growing a new head,' Santa Rosa Police Chief Mikael A. Dunbaugh said at a press conference.

One man caught up in Operation Black Widow has risked his life to speak out against the NF killing culture. Armando Frias Jr. was born into a family affiliated with the NF. At 17 he saw his best friend shot in a robbery. Later, a mentor, Chente Sanchez, received an order to kill a drug dealer who had not been paying his dues to La Nuestra Familia. The man was Sanchez's friend. Sanchez took a noble but foolhardy decision and refused the order, knowing the NF code would be enforced.

Within three weeks he was found on Pacheco Pass with a bullet in his head. Frias learned of the death in a newspaper clipping he read while he was locked up.

Initially, Frias was convinced that Chente Sanchez had sacrificed himself for a worthy cause. For a time Frias was a member of the lesser-rated street gang, Nuestra Raza, but he soon got deeply involved in the Nuestra Familia. He began selling drugs on the street and willingly became enmeshed in gang life, obedient to the orders smuggled out of Pelican Bay.

'When you make that step and you start functioning with them, there ain't no stepping back,' said Frias. 'I thought what I was doing was right.'

That's why in 2001, when he was out of jail, he shot Raymond Sanchez, a Nuestra Familia dropout who had been selling drugs in NF territory. Sanchez had repeatedly snubbed warnings to get out of the area and had refused to share his proceeds with the gang. When Frias found himself in the same bar as Sanchez he knew what he had to do. Indeed, had Frias been spotted in the same room as Sanchez without taking action he would have been branded a coward and subject to a death sentence himself. The job was done without emotion. 'The truth is, I really didn't feel nothing. The life I chose let me know those things are going to happen.' Predictably, Frias was sentenced to life. But during the long hours available to him for contemplation he began to question the gang's commitment to its own mission. 'I started seeing abuses of authority, people wanting something done for their own personal gain, not for Norteños in general,' he said.

He started seeing gang members using drugs, which is strictly against the gang's constitution. Members who had been tagged 'no good' by the leadership, theoretically a permanent label and a death sentence, were able to buy their redemption by sending money to Pelican Bay.

'I tried to feel what (Sanchez's) family was feeling,' he said. 'I put myself in their position. I can imagine what they're going through. If the same thing happened to my dad, he's my best friend, I'd go crazy. The same thing with my son.

'If I could go back and change it, I would. I wasted my life. I took a life and I've affected my son's life. And for what?

'I saw (the gang) as a movement, a cause, like Pancho Villa or Emilio Zapata or Cesar Chavez. I thought it was pure. But really it's all corrupted by greed and drugs and money.'

It finally came to light that the street general who ordered the hit carried out by

Frias, Daniel Hernandez, was in fact working for the FBI.

Now Frias only sees his young son through a pane of glass at the Monterey County Jail and can only talk to him only over the phone on the wall nearby. When he gets home, the boy picks up the phone and tries to talk to his dad again.

Frias fervently hopes his son will sidestep gang culture.

In the meantime he knows his disparaging comments about the gang will undoubtedly be noticed and could bring retribution, but he says he's not afraid.

He never expects to be paroled and intends to write a book to discourage young Latinos from the gang lifestyle. Being proud of one's heritage does not require a life of crime, he says.

A member of the Latin Kings gang in the Bronx declares his allegiance by wearing a crown as he carries his baby

Members of the Texas Syndicate gang show off their membership tattoos at Hughes Prison

Texas Syndicate

Since its inception in California's Folsom Prison, the Texas Syndicate has set out to prove itself the most violent of prison gangs. Its members are drawn from Cuban, Colombian and Mexican immigrants. Identifying tattoos are various and often the key initials TS are cleverly disguised in the artwork.

The best of the rest

New gangs and splinter groups are swift to form. They are eager to surpass in violence and ruthlessness those already in existence, like the Latin Kings, who were launched in the 1940s and are linked to East Coast prisons and to Chicago. Among the fastest growing of these new groups is Public Enemy Number One

(PEN1), which has a white supremacist agenda and is active mainly in California. Not strictly a prison gang – it boasts members and activities inside and out of jail – PEN1 activists have proved valuable in carrying out AB orders beyond prison boundaries.

Known as 'needle Nazis' because of their heavy drug use, there are an estimated 400 plus members. Unlike other gangs, there's no binding code or recognized hierarchy although certain individuals have gained a reputation of being the kingpin.

Donald Reed 'Popeye' Mazza was Public Enemy Number 1's 'shot caller'. A heavy heroin user he has a violent criminal history. One incident on his prison record amply illustrates his commitment to the gang. In April 1999, according to prosecutors, only 10 hours after being released from prison, Mazza stabbed PEN1 associate William Austin, while Dominic "Droopy" Rizzo, the number two leader in PEN1 (and godfather to Austin's child), held Austin down. Austin was a member of the Los Angeles Death Squad, another white supremacist gang, and an active participant in PEN1 and the Nazi Low Riders (NLR) activities. Austin was said to have been attacked in this 'prison-ordered hit' because fellow gang members believed he had turned informer. According to prosecutors, an Aryan Brotherhood member is believed to have overseen the attack.

In 2003 Mazza was convicted of attempted murder and is currently serving 15 years at Pelican Bay. In the summer of 2005 he reportedly earned his Aryan Brotherhood 'dancing shoes', meaning that he was inducted into the AB. Mazza's elevation into AB ranks is likely to boost PEN1's position and power in California's prison system.

Neta is a long-standing gang believed to have chapters inside and out of prisons in 36 cities across nine states. In Florida authorities have identified 240 different gangs operating within its prisons.

There has been some success in blunting the potency of the gangs. In 2002 a court heard about the activities of the Barrio Azteca (BA) in West Texas. Formed in 1986, allegedly to protect and unite all Hispanic inmates from the El Paso area, it remained under the radar despite a long-running spat with the Mexikanemi gang, which officially ended when a peace treaty was agreed in 1998.

This was, an attorney remarked, 'an extremely violent gang operating in the El Paso/Cuidad Juarez area as well as in federal correctional facilities, the state prison system and local jails. Their enterprise included extortion, assault, murder, attempted murder,

Deported back to Honduras, these 18th Street gang members retain their allegiance

money laundering and narcotics trafficking.' A civil injunction against 35 members and their associates slowed the gang's activities.

Drug money

Allegiances struck up between gangs mean that members of one often mingle with members of another. The Aryan Brotherhood will co-operate with the Mexican Mafia, the Dirty White Boys and Nazi Low Riders. Long-standing rivalries dictate that gang members occasionally target competitor gangs, seeking to beat or murder the membership. This can happen during 'cell pops', when a prison's mechanical cell doors open accidentally. Occupants are ever ready to rush out and attack nearby rivals. But while gangs claim that long-standing feuds are the cause of the violence, drugs turf wars are more generally at the heart of the problem.

Violence between gangs on the inside is infecting city and urban streets. In California the rise in crime carried out on the say-so of gang bosses in previously peaceful communities has become an issue.

'The spike in black and Latino hate crime violence is due in part to the undeclared war between blacks and Latinos that has raged in some of California's jails and prisons,'

explained Earl Ofari Hutchinson, a political analyst and social issues commentator. 'That battle has spawned an even bigger fight in poor neighborhoods between gangs over crime and drug turfs. The violence has resulted in dozens of injuries and a few deaths. There are rumors that black and Latino prison gangs have ordered hits on other blacks and Latinos on the streets as part of their turf battles.'

Keeping in touch

Just how gang leaders establish sophisticated communications networks is a matter being studied by prison authorities.

Clearly, gang barons can issue orders by telephone although calls are supposed to be monitored. With access to a phone they can make calls to members in other prisons via the 'three ways' system'. Here bosses simultaneously call a member on the outside, who holds the two phones to one another. Just as troublingly is a 1999 report by the Justice Department that found that just 3.5 per cent of all calls in federal prisons came under scrutiny. Usually, known gang leaders are kept incommunicado while in prison to illiminate the option of telephone conversations. Still they find ways of flicking the reins of power.

They can send orders to the outside through other convicts letters' home, using code to avoid detection by prison censors. Sometimes the codes are so obscure that FBI cryptologists must be called in to crack them. A few prisoners have mastered the double alphabet pioneered by Sir Francis Bacon. Organizers of La Nuestra Familia are well versed in the Huazanguillo dialect of the ancient Aztec language of Nahautl and choose to communicate in this obscure language.

Also they can send coded messages and documents, such as hit lists, inside reams of legal papers that are off limits to guards' searches, thereby using their lawyers as unwitting couriers.

Some gang bosses have written letters using urine, realizing that the words vanish when dry only to re-appear when the paper is heated. Small letters have also been secreted on the inside of envelopes where joins overlap. Notes bearing tiny writing, known as 'kites' or 'wilas', can be smuggled out of prisons in body orifices. At Pelican Bay maximum security prison a 14-page list containing the names of 1,500 Hispanic gang members was recovered from the rectum of a prisoner.

To communicate between themselves prisoners can 'fly kites'. These are minutely written notes attached to a strand of elastic pulled from the waist band of prison jumpsuits and then expertly flung into another cell.

Sometimes leaders can simply talk face-to-face in the exercise yard. Men who have been paroled are commonly used as mules to carry messages to the outside world.

Not all gangs live by the same rules, of course, but there are some common

GANG SLANG

Torpedo – hit man

Wolfpacks – recently paroled gang members with orders to carry out crimes on the streets

Carnales – soldier

Dime – taxes

Kites – messages

Rapos – rapists

Chesters – child molesters

Hotshot – lethal dose of heroin, used in assassinations

X files – rules and regulations of the Mexican Mafia

Bringing down the light – murder contract

conventions. It is usual to 'blood in – blood out' of gang membership. This means that aspirants must kill at the behest of gang leaders to win acceptance into its ranks – and that they will be killed if they choose to leave. Having killed, the new member will be expected to swear a loyalty oath that is binding, as numerous gang members have discovered to their cost.

Life and death of a gang member

Robert Viramontes, known as 'Brown Bob', spent most of his life inside California's state prisons, rising to become one of the highest-ranking members of La Nuestra Familia. After serving the NF for 20 years Viramontes opted for 'semiretirement', guaranteed, according to the NF constitution, to any member who survives two decades. In effect, it is to be the only accepted way to get out alive.

While still loyal to the NF, Viramontes began having second thoughts about the vicious lifestyle membership entailed.

Although he never spoke out against the gang or informed to police he did caution young gangsters through a program called 'Mothers Against Gangs'. Significantly, he asked tattoo artists to cover the massive 'Nuestra Familia' emblem on his back. To earn a living once out of the gang lifestyle he worked as an office cleaner and at his one-storey home where he lived with wife, Esperanza, and two sons, aged 17 and six, he took up gardening.

Indeed, he was tending his rose bushes the day his assassins called. In the early evening of 19 April 1999 a Ford Explorer carrying three young men pulled up to the kerb in front of Viramontes's home. It had been stolen from a nearby driveway.

The driver, Albert 'Beto' Avila, waited at the wheel while two men in T-shirt and shorts leapt from the passenger-side doors. The first was David 'Dreamer' Escamilla, a member of the NF who was out on parole after doing time for attempted murder. He was accompanied by Santos 'Bad Boy' Burnias, a longtime NF member who had also done a stint for

The exercise yard at Corcoran State Prison, California, is regularly patrolled by guards

attempted murder. A fourth person, Antonio 'Chuco' Guillen, the San Jose NF underboss, supervised from a car parked down the street.

Seeing his assailants, Viramontes turned toward the open garage and tried to run into his home. As he crawled towards the door, he was hit seven times in the chest, back, legs and arms. One bullet grazed his left cheek. Dreamer got so close to his target that blood splattered back onto his hands.

The murder of Robert Viramontes was, like most hits on higher-ups, ordered from inside Pelican Bay State Prison, La Nuestra Familia's headquarters. He knew his murder was on the cards and was even warned by a long-time comrade that the death sentence had been issued. In gang parlance, he could 'smell the blood' or sense the threat. If Viramontes believed his long and loyal service would help him sidestep the inevitable he was sadly mistaken.

Viramontes had been 'blooded in' to the NF in 1978 when he and some other NF members were convicted of manslaughter for hanging an inmate they thought was a snitch.

When Viramontes was first paroled from San Quentin in 1992, he returned home to the South Bay and took a tentative step toward

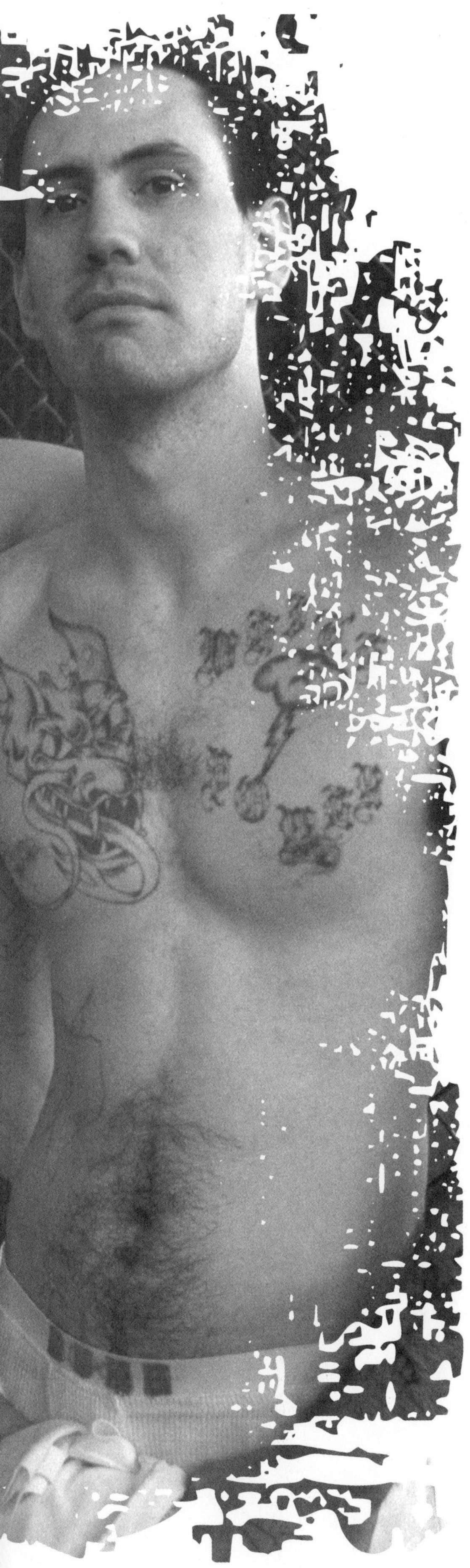

loosening ties with the NF. He approached Mothers Against Gangs about being a speaker, getting so nervous before his first presentation that he asked his family to wait outside. After each subsequent speech, he took notes on his own performance and was clearly committed to an anti-gang agenda.

At the same time, the Santa Clara County district attorney's office was engaging in a thorough and costly war against La Nuestra Familia, a clean sweep that would eventually involve Viramontes.

Eventually he was subpoenaed to testify before a grand jury, but was one of the few witnesses who refused to talk about his role in the gang. The answers he gave contradicted other sworn testimony so Viramontes was convicted of perjury and sent back to San Quentin in 1994.

Inside Viramontes came across Chuco, who was serving time for drug possession. Chuco noticed Viramontes' back, and saw a recently tattooed Aztec figure disguising his NF emblem of a large sombrero with a knife and three drops of blood. According to NF member Anthony 'Chavo' Jacobs, Viramontes's cover-up tattoo work caused Chuco to feel 'ashamed'. And when he learned Viramontes had spoken on behalf of Mothers Against Gangs, Chuco remarked: 'He's poisoning young minds.'

Unaware that doubt was being cast on his commitment, Viramontes made what proved to be two fatal mistakes. He announced he wanted to revise the gang's policy about attacks on other gangs, suggesting that NF members now 'stand their ground and act aggressively only if the enemy acts aggressively.' He then called for a truce with the NF's greatest enemy, the Mexican Mafia .

By now suspicion was rife about Viramontes and a whispering campaign circulated through the prison. The death penalty, ordered by men with whom he had once rubbed shoulders, was apparently given before he left prison. Twenty years of service and a respected constitution ultimately counted for nothing.

Codes of conduct

It is not unusual for tightly run gangs to boast a ruling council or commission. There may be

Even when not directly linked to a gang, prison tattoos can be lurid and violent, as seen here in Midway prison, Texas

a single, all powerful commander but, there will also be generals, captains and lieutenants to oversee the grisly activities of the foot soldiers. It is at this level of pseudo sophistication that corrupt prison guards are likely to be lured into co-operation.

Gang hierarchies encourage their underlings to study subjects as diverse as philosophy, military strategy and corporate management. This helps engender trust, discipline and respect.

Tattoos have long been used to denote gang membership but as prisons attempt to weed out gang power these are now being disguised.

Part of gang wealth comes from levies paid by its members or their families. Those on the outside pay substantially more than those in jail. Of course, if they falter on payments they are usually given the chance to act on behalf of the gang in a robbery or a hit to wipe out the debt. Most comply, knowing their families could be at risk if they don't.

Gang culture is also detectable in popular music. From the favelas of Sao Paulo to the back streets of Los Angeles, neighbourhoods are ringing with the sound of CDs extolling the goodness and the power of prison gangs.

This music helps to enhance the image of the gang and means that crimes ordered by gang leaders from inside their cells are not the only problem facing lawmen in big cities. Generations of disaffected young people are unduly impressed by the conduct of prison gangs and commit brutal crimes so that they can be sent to jail, to be in the company of those they admire most. And it is the young men among them, inducted as they serve their sentences, who will willingly step into the shoes of gang leaders snared by vigilant authorities.

Sociologist David Ward believes prison gang supremos achieve their status by being perceived as 'the strongest of the strong':

> 'In some quarters these would be the people who would be in combat; they would be your medal of honour winners because they would never give in, they would never give up. Their strength under circumstances in which all the rest of us would have folded long ago is something that really is extraordinary. I don't say this in a way of admiration as much as in a way of wondering how people can survive this kind of regime forever.'

Prison cells are often the place where young men are inducted into gangs and their culture

Getting out

By committing known gang members to the Security Housing Unit in Supermax prisons the

authorities hoped to smother their power. The policy appears to have failed.

One man who joined a white gang learned his criminal trade after being sent to the SHU.

'I always looked at the SHU as like a piece of steel that you could sharpen yourself with. You're not going to get that kind of opportunity to look at who you are and what you need to change about yourself to be stronger like you will in the SHU.

'All I was waiting for was someone who was in trouble so I could stab them. That's all I looked forward to.

'I think that it's hard for normal people to understand but the way I used to look at prison when I was younger was like it was a kind of college. I had to

It is thought that all inmates at the Chalatenango prison in El Salvador are members of the Mara 18 gang

go there to further myself. If I wanted a career in what I was doing then I needed to go to prison and make a name for myself in there in order to do so.

'By all standards my whole philosophy was wrong. But I thought that by creating my own system of morality, that by living within the codes of the prison, doing what's right in there, being respected in there, that I had created my own society.'

In addition to those who aspire to join prison gangs there are those who join after being preyed upon by existing members who have little to lose. Given the monotony of life in a SHU, it's easy to succumb to the apparent advantages of gang membership.

In some ways, gang members found guilty of ordering crimes in the outside world are beyond punishment. Typically, they are already serving life terms in the harshest prison regime the US can offer. There's little that can make a real difference to their torpid daily routine and the gang masters know this. Extra years added to the end of a sentence seem meaningless to those who know they are likely to die in jail.

Choosing a different route to undermine gang supremacy, some prisons offer disenchanted or desperate men the chance to leave both a gang and the SHU through a process called debriefing. Some states offer the reformed gang member a route out of the Supermax and into anonymity and ordinary prison once gang membership has been renounced. However, at Pelican Bay the exit from the SHU could have an unacceptably high price. It involves snitching on other gang members, for which the penalty may be death. In a debrief lasting several hours the inmate is expected to spill all he knows about gang life in and out of jail, including the names of the major players.

At Pelican Bay there is a unit for former gang members, kept segregated from the other prisoners – for they are acknowledged as marked men by prison authorities and prison gangs alike. Here they can enjoy being outside without handcuffs for the first time since entering the SHU. Classes in computer skills, victim awareness and anger management are at last available. It's a pivotal part of rejoining society. But some prisoner welfare groups are opposed to the debriefing ideal, believing prisoners should not be encouraged to put themselves at risk as informers.

And, as one informer put it:

> 'I've burned my bridges. There are no more bridges. When you take that step you're done. Period. There's no going back. And you'd better hope that nobody catches you because if they do then you're going to become another statistic.'

The debriefing process is certainly not providing an answer to the problem of prison gangs. The majority are deterred by the stigma attached to being an informer. And for every reformed character there are untold numbers of new recruits waiting in the wings.

At the moment the solution to the perils of prison gangs is unknown. El Salvador pursues a policy of jailing any known associate of a prison gang. This merely has the effect of concentrating membership within easy reach of the gang masters.

SOUTH AFRICA

NUMBERS ADDING UP

In South Africa the authorities can do little in the face of powerful 'number gangs'. The lure of the gangs is so great that members prefer to be inside prison, where they get free medical care, a bed, food and the respect that gang membership brings. These benefits are not always available in the slums outside jail.

There are three number gangs, the 26s, the 27s and the 28s. Generally speaking, the 26s are linked to robberies and cash accumulation, the 27s are associated with blood-letting while the top-of-the-pile 28s are known for sexual domination. The subtext with regard to the 28s is that young men sent to prison to await trial are likely to be raped their first night behind bars and as a result may well contract HIV/Aids. The only liberation from gang life is death.

South Africa's biggest prison is Pollsmoor, 25 miles from Cape Town and where Nelson Mandela was held for a time during the Apartheid era. Built for 4,000 inmates, it usually holds at least double that number and up to 60 men might share a cell designed for only 18. There is only one toilet and obviously not enough beds to go around.

Although estimates vary there is thought to be just one warden for every hundred prisoners. This means that access to recreational and educational facilities is limited. All depends on the availability of staff.

It also explains why prisoners enjoy various unofficial privileges, including drugs and porn. There simply aren't enough staff to crack down. Wardens also tread warily around gang members as recruits frequently earn their stripes by wounding or killing prison personnel. Staff who have upset gang hierarchies are targeted. Sometimes wardens learn that an attack against them has been ordered yet they must continue working, not knowing where or when they may be attacked.

On arrival prisoners are fingerprinted and subjected to a strip search during which they must squat to prove they are not carrying drugs anally. At this stage existing gang members, with their razor and ink tattoos, are swiftly identifiable. High-ranking members have stars tattooed like epaulettes on their shoulders.

An expert on the number gangs at Pollsmoor is British actor Ross Kemp. Although better known as a soap opera star, in

Inmates at Pollsmoor Prison in Cape Town, South Africa, pictured leaving the polling station during the 2004 elections

> ‘OUR PRISONS are stuffed full of people who have a hatred of the prison administration, a hatred of America and have nothing but time to seethe about it. Often times they want a way to lash out or feel important. They are very likely to join groups that facilitate that anger. Anti-American feelings help all sorts of gangs recruit in prison.’
>
> — Robert Fosen, former assistant commissioner of New York state prisons

2006 he became a roving reporter for a documentary about gangs, shown on Sky television, which included a trip to Pollsmoor.

‘It is like entering a human zoo,’ he said. ‘The smells, sights and sounds are overwhelming and I don’t mind admitting, I’m frightened.’

Nonetheless, once inside he roamed the security wings and entered cells containing South Africa’s most deadly prisoners. For a while he came up against the strict code of silence that governs the numbers gangs. Infringements usually bring about a dire punishment. But eventually he earned their trust and learned about the perils of Pollsmoor, especially its dark and violent undercurrents.

Ultimately he interviewed John Mongrel, the highest ranking 28 in the prison at that time, to learn more about the sexual initiation that takes place. Mongrel was given a nine-year sentence for murder at the age of 14. But offences committed in jail mean he has not yet been released. He himself entered the 28s by stabbing another prisoner through the heart soon after arriving in prison.

Now he orders other would-be gang members to commit murder or maiming and will go along to watch it take place.

And for those who don’t go down the road of violence there’s the alternative path, sexual submission. Mongrel forces new inmates to have sex – they submit through fear and the unspoken threat of violence – although he denies being homosexual.

‘I’m a man. He is a woman or wifey. He must wash my clothes. I give him food and I give him a bed,’ Mongrel told Kemp.

Sex has been part of 28 culture virtually since its formation in 1906 when black prisoners first banded together, claiming that the prime motivation was to protect themselves from whites.

Magadien Wentzel was a leading member of the 28s gang before turning his back on the gang to write a book revealing its activities in 2004

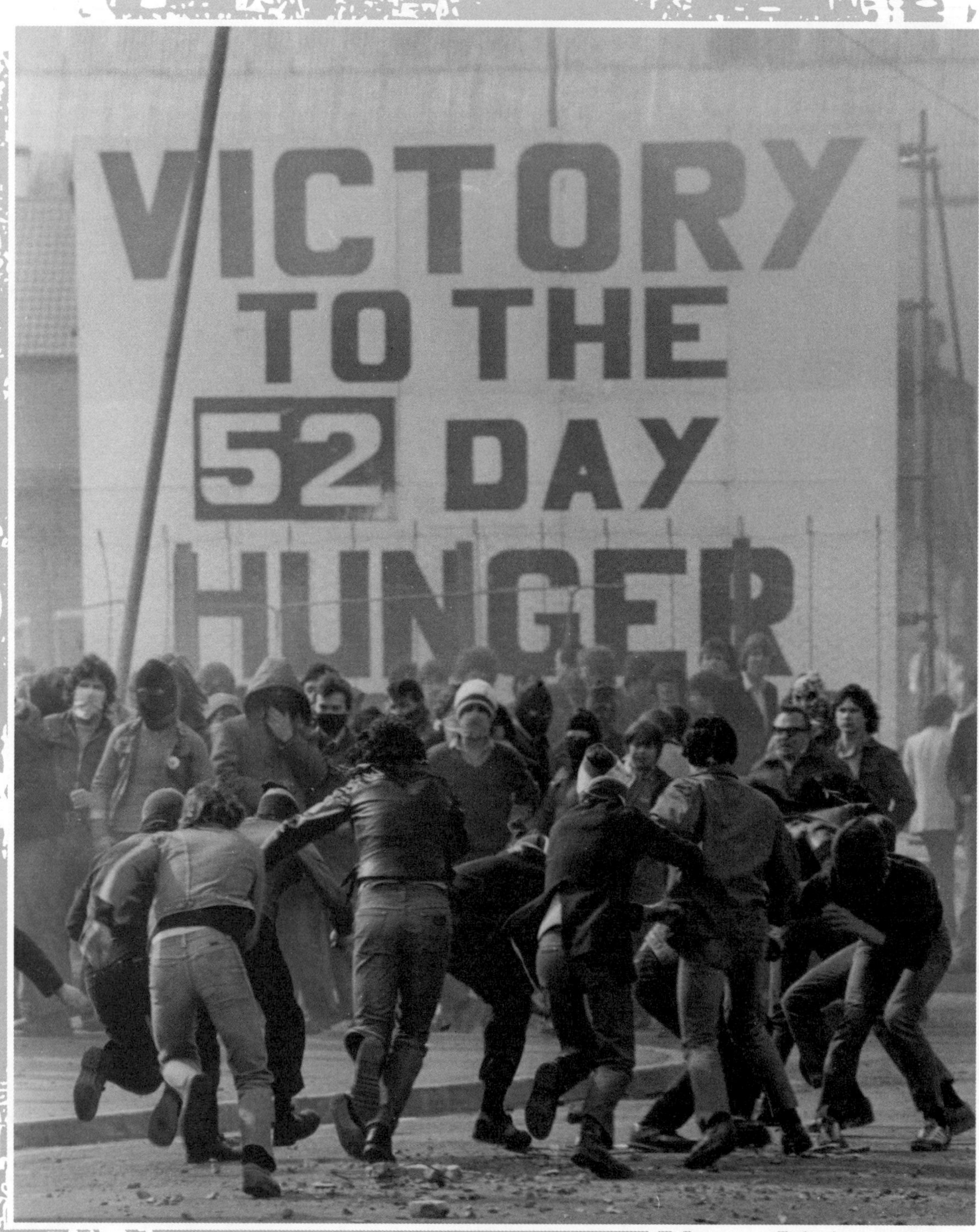

Rioters in Belfast in 1981 show their support for IRA hunger strikers in prison

Sex and drugs

An estimated 65 per cent of inmates in South African jails currently participate in sexual activity of one kind or another – and none consider themselves homosexual. Indeed, consensual same-sex relationships are frowned on in prison gang culture.

In prison sex is about power rather than sexual fulfilment and may involve 80 per cent of those awaiting trial. Rape is, said one inmate, 'an every night, every day occurrence.' Those who cannot afford gang protection, are unable to pay debts or return favours or are disinclined to violence use sex as a currency.

Sexual activity behind bars inevitably has an effect on the outside. Victims of male rape in jail often try to regain their manhood by raping women or even children when they return to their communities. Protection against sexually transmitted diseases isn't used in either instance and so HIV/AIDS is rampant.

Five years previously BBC reporter Allan Little went behind the scenes at Pollsmoor Prison and discovered the same violent, sexually-charged scenario.

He met Mogamat Benjamin, an inmate for 34 years and veteran of many violent excesses. Not only has he beheaded corpses, he has, he claims, cut out the victims' hearts and eaten them in a ritualistic bid to claim their life force.

'I am powerful,' Mogamat bragged to Little.

> 'I am partly God. No man has a higher rank in Pollsmoor than me. In the camp of the 28s a person's life is in my hands. The final decision is mine. There are people who I said should be killed and they were killed.'

Although every numbers gang is distinct – the 27s were formed as a direct response to the sexual preoccupation of the 28s – each is linked to the others by the twin threads of violence and strict ritual. It is, it seems, possible to move between the groups but only after carrying out some prescribed and horribly violent act. Those who are in the 27s act as intermediaries between the 26s and the 28s, who are generally prohibited from contacting each other. There remains a healthy mix of respect and suspicion between the three.

One man, Magadien Wentzel, was the subject of an enlightening biography that revealed the view from the inside. He outlined the aspects of violence most admired by gang members.

> 'The brave part is not the stabbing. It is what happens to you after that. Because they are going to beat the s**t out of you. And if you cry out, just once, the stabbing means nothing: you have failed. After they have f***ed you up, they are going to put you in a dark cell, with not enough food, for a long time. And if you go mad in there, if you come out crying like a baby, the stabbing means nothing.'

Gang members at Pollsmoor are so institutionalized that many would prefer to commit a fresh crime behind bars or confess to something they didn't do rather than face life with all its uncertainties on the outside.

Until the mid-1980s the numbers gangs existed only in prisons and the streets were left in the hands of different, equally violent, gangs. However, keen to cash in on the drugs trade that took off at the time, each numbers gang has aligned itself with equivalents on the outside to reap the rewards of drug involvement, including cash and drugs supply.

IRELAND

IRISH STEW

Over 25 years the activities of two rival political factions degenerated into gangsterism. One prison became an especially potent symbol of the era. It held men from both sides of the divide and placed the guards, whose thankless task was to supervise them, at huge risk. The place was Northern Ireland. The rival factions were the Irish Republican Army (IRA) and the Ulster Volunteer Force (UVF), along with their numerous offshoots with various identities. The prison in question was the distinctively-shaped Maze.

At first it was better known as Long Kesh, a disused Royal Air Force base near Lisburn.

Since 1971, when the government of Northern Ireland tried to clear the province of terrorist activity by arresting suspected IRA sympathizers and detaining them without charge, the Maze's Nissan huts have been home to a long line of terrorists.

This, it turns out, wasn't the smartest move the authorities could make as the Maze soon gained a reputation for being a 'University of Terror'.

The Maze Prison in Northern Ireland, home to a long line of terrorists

One former Republican prisoner recalled: 'We went in bad terrorists and came out good terrorists. We learned how to strip and handle weapons, how to make booby-trap bombs, how to stand up to interrogation and, basically, how to be a professional terrorist.'

For a while prisoners were given special status by the government, reflecting the political nature of their crimes. They had free association, extra visits and were excused from penal work. However, when this status was scrapped in 1976 Republican prisoners began an orchestrated campaign designed to cause maximum embarrassment to the British government, which by now governed Northern Ireland direct from London.

Dirty protest

At first they refused to wear prison uniforms and went naked, wrapping themselves in rough, prison-issue blankets. When this had no effect they refused to use toilet facilities, smearing the cell walls with faeces in a 'dirty protest'. The brand new H-blocks at the Maze were transformed into cell hells.

By 1980 Republicans began a different approach to garner national and international support. A number of inmates went on hunger strike, hoping that the threat of prisoner deaths in custody would squeeze concessions out of the British government. To the delight of Republicans, one of the hunger strikers, Bobby Sands, aged 27, was even elected to the British parliament, thus further highlighting the campaign.

But by the time Bobby Sands died of starvation, 66 days after he began his hunger strike, there was still nothing on the table from the government. A further nine prisoners died before a tacit move by the authorities brought an end to the hunger strikes. Critics argued that special status was ultimately restored in all but name.

Lost in the Maze

Nonetheless, there remained palpable tensions inside the prison walls. There were numerous escape attempts, the most successful being on 23 September 1983 when 38 Republican prisoners hi-jacked a prison meals lorry and

A 1974 photo of Michael Stone, a UFF man who went on to kill a known three Catholics during the Troubles in Northern Ireland

smashed through security gates. One prison officer, James Ferris, died of a heart attack after one of the inmates held a home-made knife to his throat.

One of the least successful attempts occurred the following year when Loyalist Benjamin Redfern stowed away aboard a waste disposal lorry. He died when the driver switched on the rubbish crushing mechanism without realizing there was an additional passenger on board.

The Maze was again in the spotlight following the 1997 murder of 37-year-old Billy Wright, a prominent and controversial Loyalist who had survived six death sentences issued by the Republicans and who predicted that he would meet his end at their hands. He was also a target for Loyalists dismayed by his uncompromising approach. When Wright was jailed on perjury charges members of the Irish National Liberation Army decided to wreak revenge on behalf of the Catholics he had previously targeted. As he waited inside a prison van before a visit three men clambered over a roof from a neighbouring yard and, using pistols smuggled into the prison, shot Wright in the heart and the lungs. Afterwards the killers calmly turned over the weapons to a Catholic priest and gave themselves up.

Peace initiatives gained momentum as the 21st century approached and by 2000 the last 'terrorist' prisoners were released from the Maze as part of the ground-breaking Good Friday Agreement, which had been arduously fashioned to bring peace to the province. One of the last men to gain his freedom was Michael Stone, a Loyalist whose crimes included shooting three mourners at a funeral.

Partial demolition of the Maze prison, a focus for hatred, was begun in October 2006.

A group of prisoners with more than 100 years' collective experience of being inside US jails drew up the *Prisoners' Handbook*. Here's a brief insight into what they said.

- ❑ Never share a cell with a friend.
- ❑ Be tolerant of your cellmate's toilet habits.
- ❑ Try to give your cellmate an hour of solitude each day and expect the same in return.
- ❑ Don't rifle through your cellmate's belongings.
- ❑ Don't blab about your cellmate to others.
- ❑ Don't criticize his personal habits – you've got bad habits too.
- ❑ Insist your cellmate keeps his diseases to himself.
- ❑ Keep the volume of radios or TVs to a minimum.
- ❑ Mind your own business.
- ❑ Don't steal from other prisoners.
- ❑ Don't pass comments on other prisoners' families.
- ❑ Don't brag.
- ❑ Help your fellow prisoner. Don't just school him in the art of the crime that happens to be your specialty. Also, see if you can teach him basic skills like reading and writing.
- ❑ Avoid faggots.
- ❑ Fight the system not other prisoners.
- ❑ Be your own man and don't join gangs, cliques or 'in-crowds'.
- ❑ Don't snitch.
- ❑ Insist on the health treatment to which you are entitled.
- ❑ Survive and get free.
- ❑ Do one day at a time. It's an old cliché but it's true. Live for today. Chances are that tomorrow will come.

"We went in bad terrorists and came out good terrorists. We learned how to strip and handle weapons, how to make booby-trap bombs, how to stand up to interrogation and, basically, how to be a professional terrorist."

3 PITCHERS & PUNKS

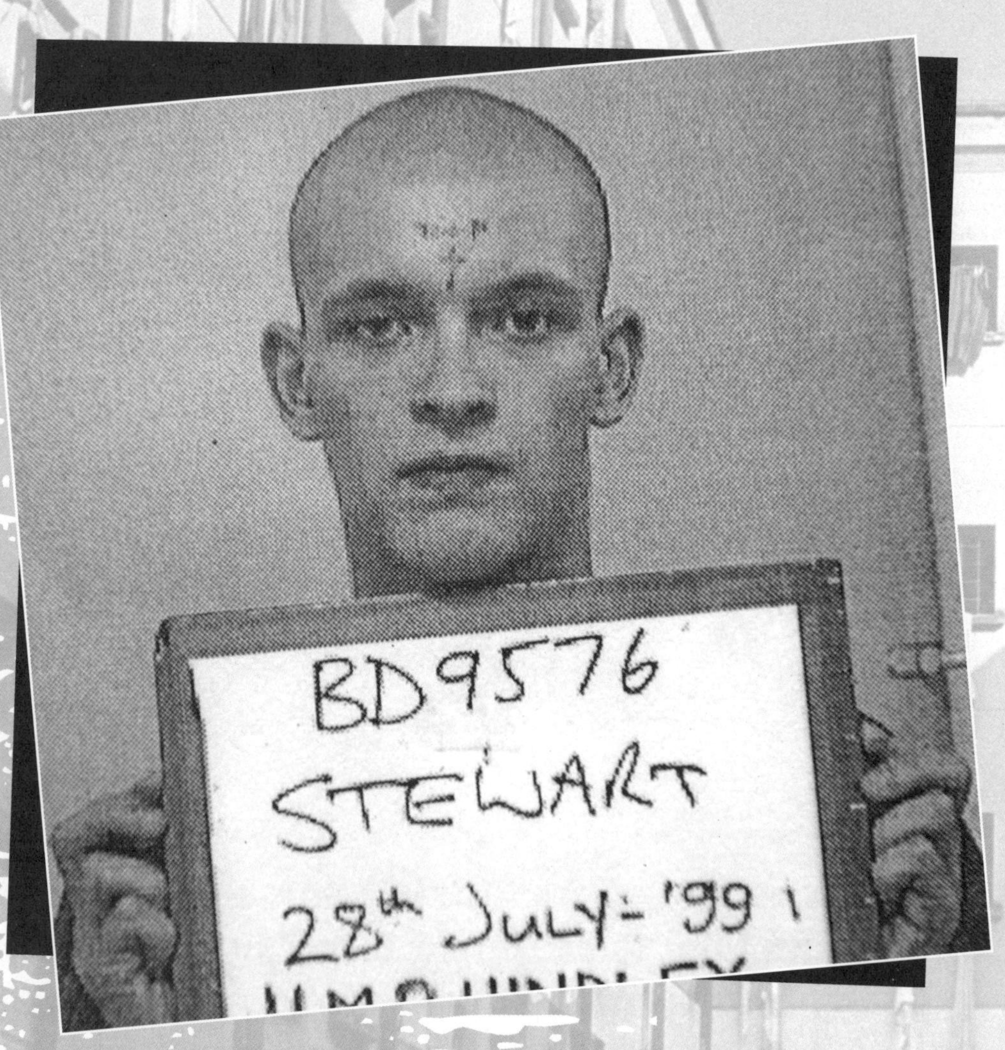

FOR some repeat offenders prison becomes a way of life. There are those, however, who are not tough enough to endure the harsh realities of an existence behind bars, whose emotional armour is swiftly pierced and whose ego subsequently drowns in the cesspool of prison life. For them prison becomes a way of death.

Suicide is part of the seamy underbelly of incarceration. Add to that illicit sex and corrupt guards and you have a fairly complete picture of the very worst facets of prison life. This murky arena is frequently ignored by commentators because of its sheer unpleasantness.

Given the hideous happenings swilling about in the prison system, is it possible that prisoner families – innocent of any crime – can remain untouched? These are desperate people who already feel their voices go unheard. Are they merely flotsam tossed around on the tide of justice or is there a route to empowerment?

Let down by the system that was supposed to be protecting as well as confining him, Rodney Hulin hanged himself in his cell, due to abuse by fellow prisoners

When he was 16-years-old Rodney Hulin and his brother set fire to an overflowing dumpster in their neighbourhood. Doused in a matter of moments the blaze caused little damage and no one was hurt. But the results of the prank were to have far-reaching effects and Rodney ultimately paid for the misdemeanour with his life.

Weary of roguish behaviour by the young, the courts decided to make an example of Rodney and sentenced him to eight years for arson. As if that wasn't bad enough, he was ordered to spend his time behind bars in an adult correctional institution.

Although he was 17 by the time he reached the Clemens Unit in Brazoria County, Texas, he stood just 5 ft 2 in tall and weight about 125 pounds. He was easy meat for predatory inmates and, within a week, he had been raped.

'Please Sir, help me'

In an attempt to be moved to a safe place Hulin wrote to the prison warden. 'I have been sexually and physically assaulted several times by several inmates. I am afraid to go to sleep, to shower and just about everything else. I am afraid that when I am doing these things I might die at any minute.' He finished the letter with the poignant plea, 'Please Sir, help me.'

Rodney Hulin, Snr gave evidence at a hearing following his son's death: '[Aged seventeen] my son was raped and sodomized by an inmate. The doctor found two tears in his rectum and ordered an HIV test, since up to a third of the 2,200 inmates there were HIV positive. Fearing for his safety, he requested to be placed in protective custody, but his request was denied because, as the warden put it, "Rodney's abuses didn't meet the 'emergency grievance' criteria."

'For the next several months, my son was repeatedly beaten by the older inmates, forced to perform oral sex, robbed, and beaten again. Each time, his requests for protection were denied by the warden. The abuses, meanwhile, continued. On the night of January 26, 1996 – seventy-five days after my son entered Clemens – Rodney attempted suicide by hanging himself in his cell. He could no longer stand to live in continual terror. It was too much for him to handle.'

Even though medical reports proved Hulin's claims his request was denied. In a second letter to the warden he again said he feared for his life. 'I have been threatened, jumped and nearly stabbed many times.' Once again, his request to be put in a safe place was turned down.

His mother, Linda Bruntmyer, finishes the story. 'On the night of 26 January 1996 my son hanged himself in his cell. He was seventeen and afraid and ashamed and hopeless. He laid in a coma for the next four months before he died.'

Rodney left a suicide note to explain his action. 'Since I was placed in prison I have found myself to be more mentally and emotionally destroyed than I have ever been. I'm very sorry to end my life this way. But if I don't do this someone will. I'm saying I'd rather die of my own free will than be killed.'

BITCH SYSTEM

Hulin was not a victim of gang culture but of the pecking order that exists in prisons. The population divides into predators, also known as pitchers, top dogs or booty bandits, and victims, otherwise called catchers, punks or June bugs. This does not generally reflect the sexuality of those involved but rather centres on issues of power and control.

Although he felt isolated by his experiences Hulin was not alone. A survey carried out in seven Midwest prisons in the 1990s found that 21 per cent of inmates had been pressed into having sex while one in ten had been raped. Once rape or sexual assault occurs, of course, it is likely to be repeated. Victims who become 'snitches' are physically threatened, so few make waves with officialdom.

For some, the prison 'bitch' system is a way of life. One man, known only as Stephen, has written about his experience of being jailed in Florida for the theft of a sleeping bag. Like Rodney he was small in stature.

Marriage and make up

'By the time I made it to prison I was known as Stephanie. I made a very rapid transition to being an alternative woman, probably

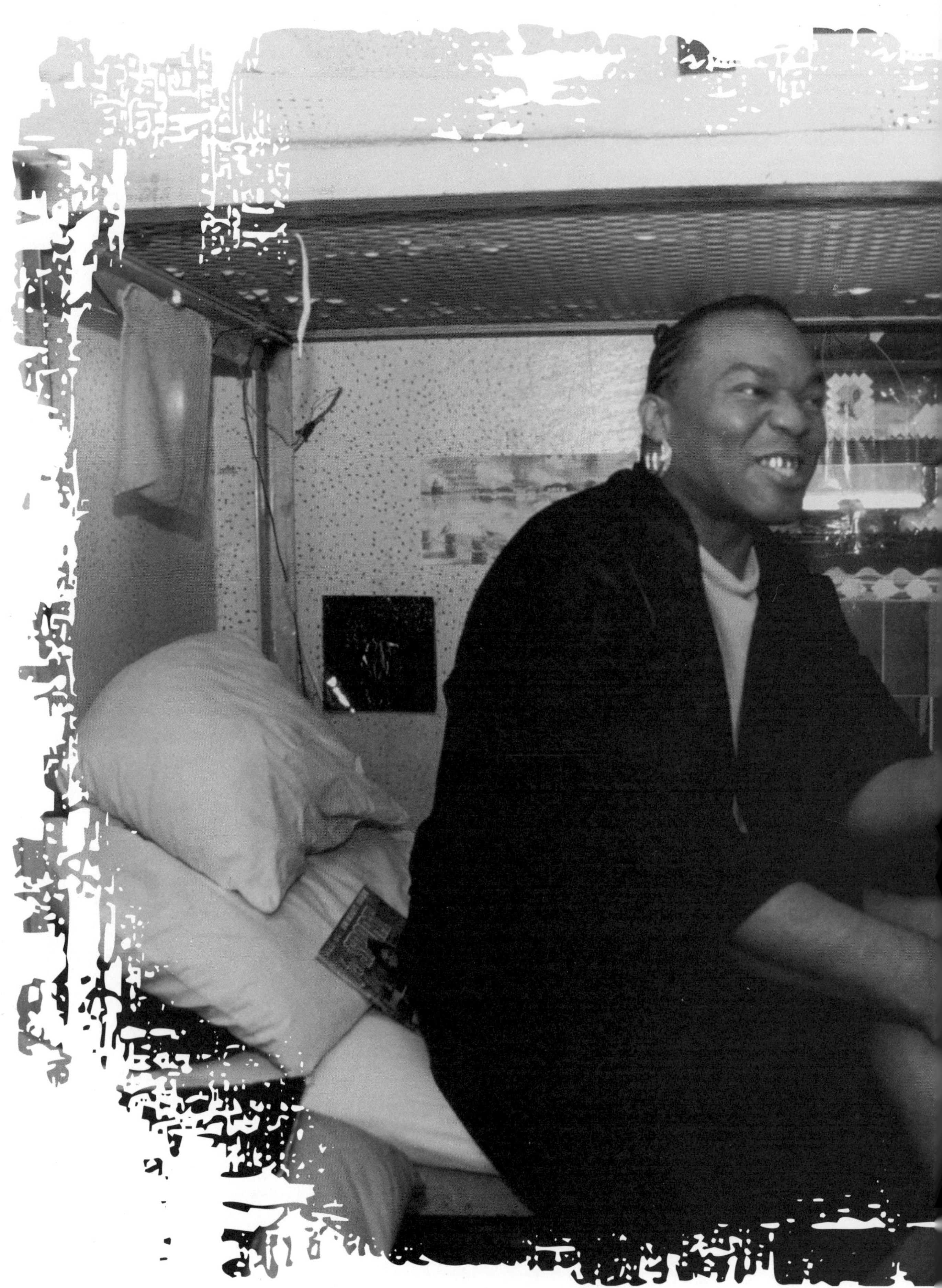

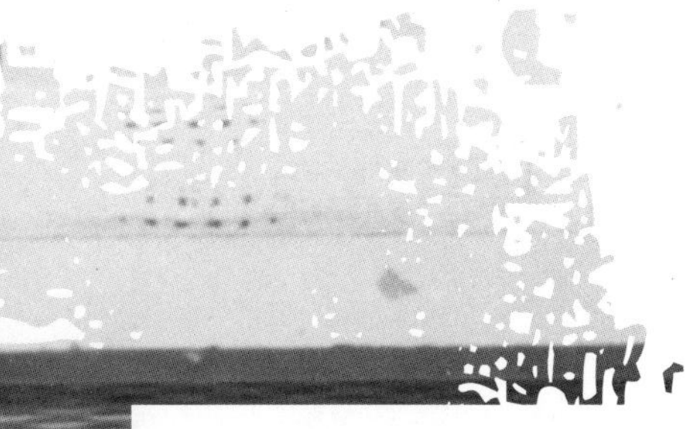

because I was simply unable to defend myself. I had never really been in a fight and was not the slightest bit tough.

'The only way that a person can be reasonably safe from

"I made a very rapid transition to being an alternative woman, probably beacuse I was unable to defend myself."

'Jackie', a gay inmate at Buckingham County prison in Virginia, talks about his experiences

assault is to acquire a reputation. Often this is done by stabbing someone. If one is successful, it can mean additional time in prison. It can also get one killed. Some people are willing to pay this price. For me, it just didn't seem like an option.

'What happens when you're sexually victimized in prison? In my case, besides using a feminine version of my name, I began shaving my legs and other body hair, and wearing female attire and make-up. As the abuse went on unabated for several years my original identity seemed to disintegrate.'

He confessed to using Kool-Aid to make pigment for eye shadow and lipstick, making sexy underwear from old T shirts and, under duress, taking vows with a cellmate in a travesty of the wedding service.

Therapist Steven Braveman, of Monterey, California, offers insight into the after-effects felt by prisoners forced into same-gender sex. 'They are deeply ashamed but cannot talk about it. They often think it's their own fault and turn to drugs and alcohol to numb the pain. They may act out their sexual victimization on others or turn to anonymous sex or just shut down sexually. We are talking about thousands of deeply traumatized men coming out of our prisons back into our society,' he said.

An old story

It's not a new trend, either. J. J. Maloney served time in a jail in Missouri before becoming a prize-winning journalist specializing in crime and justice systems. More than 40 years ago he wrote about the difficulties facing rookie prisoners.

'No matter how much you've been around, you feel uneasy when you go to prison. If you are young and good-looking, you can count on being confronted again and again. If you have money, there will be people who want it. If you are helpless, there are people who will try to make a reputation at your expense. Or you may simply say the wrong thing to the wrong person.

'In 1961 a prisoner I knew went up to a 22-year-old man and told him that he wanted to have sex with him. The young convict, within two months of going home on a two-year sentence, replied, "I don't want any trouble but I'm not going to be a punk." (A punk plays the female role in a homosexual relationship.)

'The young man worked on the food service dock. The next day the older inmate walked up, drove a 22-inch ice pick through the young man and raped him as he lay dying.

'In 1963 a 16-year-old black inmate resisted the sexual advances of a group of older convicts. They caught him in the A-hall shower and stabbed him to death while he screamed for help. After they killed him they rolled his body up in a tarpaulin, dried themselves off and returned to their cells. All because he didn't want to be a punk.

'Some older inmates decided they were going to make a punk out of another young black

The communal shower room at Limestone Correctional Facility, Alabama

A prisoner who has passed out while seated in a restraining chair

convict at Jeff City. The boy's uncle, also serving time in the prison, tried to intercede on his behalf. The uncle was stabbed to death for "meddling".'

Fringe benefits

If sex becomes a currency behind bars it's not just convicts who use it. There have been numerous instances of prison guards having sex with inmates, usually in women's prisons where there are plenty of men on the payroll.

For nearly a decade prison guard Michael Everett conducted an affair with Angela Curtis, an inmate in the prison where he worked. In July 2004, two days after being questioned about their relationship, the 53-year-old Everett walked into his front garden in Coldwater, Michigan, and shot himself in the head.

Curtis – who kept explicit love letters from Everett – explained that the affair got underway in 1992 after he eliminated details of a misconduct charge from her file.

'It was just a barter for sex,' Curtis said. 'I was young, I was very scared, and all I wanted was to go home. If I had that ticket on my record, I would have been flopped for parole. If it took exchanging sex with a guard [to get home], that's what you did.'

The relationship was consensual, she confirmed. 'In my mind it was exciting. He had power as an officer, and he could do things for me to make it easier for me to do my time,' she said.

It was also barely hidden and many people, including his superiors, were aware of what was going on. 'It's such a closed environment (in prison); everybody knows everybody's business. There is no way to hide anything inside those walls.' Guards even acted as lookouts while sex acts were in progress. Apart from her cell, she had sex with him in classrooms, laundry rooms – indeed, every time the opportunity arose.

'Women in prison have issues and are very needy,' she said. 'Most have drug problems or emotional problems from prior abuse.'

If you are helpless, there are people who will try to make a reputation at your expense. Or you may simply say the wrong thing to the wrong person.

At the time she was vulnerable because she was still mourning for her first husband, who died in 1990, the year before she went to prison. Despite promising to look after her when she was released, Curtis heard nothing from Everett after she walked through the prison gates.

Prison authorities have taken steps to eliminate guard/inmate relationships by removing cupboard doors and assigning women guards to one-on-one duties with prisoners. However, most women's prisons tend to be medium or low security so they are not infested with security cameras. With prison guards in a position of power and inmates desperate for extra privileges the division between consensual and coercion is blurred and it is a difficult problem to eradicate. There have been numerous instances of women prisoners becoming pregnant after starting jail terms.

The guard's armoury

There are other reasons why inmates might come to fear prison officers in America. For a start, most are armed. In addition to wielding a baton, prison officers in the US may carry Taser guns and pepper spray. Indeed, Tasers are a weapon of choice among both prison guards and police. Usually resembling a pistol, it fires two darts that can penetrate up to two inches (five cm) of clothing from a distance of 21 feet to deliver a shock on the order of 50,000 volts.

The charge, which lasts five seconds or less, causes muscle spasm and paralysis. The T-waves work by overwhelming the body's electrical system, in effect suspending the nervous system. Victims are rendered helpless and invariably curl up in an effort to protect themselves, making it safe for guards to approach.

Obviously, the main advantage of Tasers is that they remove the need for firearms. Troublemakers can be efficiently targeted and by-standers are not put at risk. There have, however, been numerous questions over whether they are the cause of unexplained deaths. In 1989 a Canadian study showed that Taser guns used as cattle prods induced heart attacks in cows. Yet hundreds of police officers have volunteered to take Taser blasts during trials and none, as far as is known, have died.

Prison guards also use pepper spray to subdue violent inmates. Pepper spray – also known as OC (oleoresin capsicum) spray – is derived from hot chili peppers and was originally developed for riot control and as a defense against marauding wild bears. It causes tears, pain and temporary blindness. Anyone who comes into contact with it will immediately shut their eyes and they quickly becomes incapacitated. The spray also affects the mucous membranes in the nose, throat and sinuses. Victims fear that they will choke on their own saliva as the irritant overwhelms the normal body responses. Water provides little or no relief although washing with mild detergents may help. The pain lasts on average for about 45 minutes and skin can be horribly

Unchained Melody was the theme music of *Unchained*, a 1955 film about prison life, starring former footballer Elroy 'Crazylegs' Hirsch. The music was by Alex North and the lyrics by Hy Zaret. Although the film soon sank into obscurity the tune became a hit in the fifties, eighties, nineties and again in 2003. It was also something of an anthem for prisoners involved in the bitch system. This fact was presumably unknown to Queen Elizabeth II, who was serenaded with the song by fans at Buckingham Palace in 2002 on the 50th anniversary of her coronation.

scarred if it comes into close contact with the spray.

Once again, the advantage of pepper spray is that nobody dies from a stray bullet. However, its effects are usually felt not only by the target of the spray but by those in cells nearby. Even prisoners in different corridors can detect its use by a prickling in the throat and involuntary tears.

Prison guards have been known to use leashed dogs in certain instances, including cell searches.

Problematic prisoners may also be detained in a restraint chair. This is a chair with straps for the arms and legs that prevent prisoners from lashing out. A special net is usually slipped over their heads to stop them spitting. Anyone needing a spell in the restraint chair is usually hog-tied, with both wrists and ankles tied together, so that they can be more easily carried and placed in the chair. If the handcuffs are not removed before the prisoner is strapped into the restraint chair there is a real danger of positional asphyxiation.

Use of force

There's no question that prison officers sometimes have to use force to control inmates. Judge Thelton Henderson, who was in charge of a 1996 court case that focused on the shortcomings of Pelican Bay Prison, recognized this.

> 'Perhaps the paramount responsibility of prison administrators is to maintain the safety and security of both staff and inmates... Prison officials have the unenviable task of keeping dangerous men in safe custody under humane conditions. There is no question that this demanding and often thankless undertaking will require prison staff to use force against inmates. Indeed, responsible deployment of force is not only justifiable on many occasions, but absolutely necessary to maintain the security of the institution. As one expert at trial succinctly stated, when it comes to force it is "as dangerous to use too little as it is to use too much".'

But there remains a suspicion that sometimes the prison guard's response gets out of hand and this has been cited in numerous law suits brought by prisoners or their families.

Silent treatment

Beyond the brandishing of weapons and use of restraints though there's a troubling culture that has surfaced in California's Department of Correction.

Since the investigation into the prison at Pelican Bay a 'code of silence' among California prison officers has been recognized. The code means that staff will not talk about abuses against inmates – or other officers – no matter how sadistic or illegal. In his findings at the time Judge Henderson observed:

'Several prison staff admitted to a code of silence problem. . . We also observed at trial that prison staff frequently could not recall the identity of other staff whom they testified did or said certain things, although other details were easily recalled. Prison staff also report to internal investigators, with notable frequency, that they had just looked the other way, been distracted by something else, or had their visibility impaired at the moment the alleged misuse of force was

Guards being briefed at Gatesville prison, Texas

said to have occurred. . . . Those who violate the code of silence risk hostility from other prison staff.'

Green Wall

Clearly, inmates are at increased risk if those responsible for their welfare turn a blind eye in times of stress. But the code of silence has had even more far-reaching effects upon prison guards than inmates, especially for 'whistle-blowers', those who have flagged up wrong-doers in the system.

California state law protects the identity of whistleblowers. However, that meant nothing for Donald 'DJ' Vodicka when a report fingering fellow prison officers for illicit membership in a gang was leaked at Salinas Valley State Prison.

Vodicka, a highly respected officer and member of the Investigative Services Unit, was asked by superiors to investigate rumours about the gang known as the Green Wall. He discovered a closely knit group, formed in or about 1998 after a Thanksgiving Day riot and a number of attacks upon prison officers, which was rooted in solidarity and camaraderie. Within a few years, however, its members graduated to fresh excesses and were guilty of intimidating both inmates and colleagues in the same style as the illegal prison gangs.

Green Wall members were brutal towards inmates, frequently beating them and planting incriminating evidence during cell searches. Guards who witnessed these abuses were also threatened. Anyone who broke the code of silence was subject to savage retaliation, both during and outside work, through open hostility, violence and vandalism of property.

The Green Wall refers to the colour of officers' uniforms. Its members flash gang signs to each other, spread graffiti and decorate personal items with the emblems 'GW' or '7/23' – G and W are the seventh and 23rd letters in the alphabet. They were said to drink green beer and present one another with green-handled knives in honour of their association.

In a lawsuit filed against the state, Vodicka alleges that after he blew the whistle on the Green Wall he became the target of retaliation by co-workers and superior officers. He was accused in front of prisoners of being a snitch, which put his safety in jeopardy. Later he wore a bullet-proof vest, carried a hidden weapon and said he feared for his life. Even after transferring to a new prison he was unable to resume a normal existence. Someone contacted his new colleagues and told them what he had done. Once again, he was publicly and humiliatingly branded a rat. And he didn't get any help from his union, the California Correctional Peace Officers Association (CCPOA), even though he had paid his dues. He ultimately quit the prison service, citing a stress-related illness.

CCPOA Vice President Lance Corcoran said investigations and allegations concerning the Green Wall and officer abuse of inmates have been circulating around Salinas Valley for five years but are far from proven. 'It's sexy, it sounds good, but nobody's really shown anything,' Corcoran said. Corcoran said when Salinas Valley first opened, 80 per cent to 90 per cent of its staff was relatively inexperienced

Top Ten Prison Films

- ❑ **The Shawshank Redemption (1994)** starring Tim Robbins, about life behind bars in a tough prison for an unlikely prisoner.
- ❑ **Midnight Express (1978)** starring Brad Davis, about life in a Turkish jail for a convicted US drug pedlar.
- ❑ **Cool Hand Luke (1967)** starring Paul Newman, about the pressures brought to bear on a rebel convict.
- ❑ **The Green Mile (1999)** starring Tom Hanks, concerning the life and death of an unusual prisoner.
- ❑ **Scum (1979)** starring Ray Winstone, about life and riots in a British borstal, the old style youth offenders institute.
- ❑ **The Big House (1930)** starring Robert Montgomery; a man must adapt to life in prison after being convicted of drunk driving.
- ❑ **Papillon (1973)** starring Steve McQueen; an escape artist weighs up life on Devil's Island.
- ❑ **Stir Crazy (1980)** starring Richard Pryor and Gene Wilder; an irreverent look a life inside.
- ❑ **The Longest Yard (1974)** starring Burt Reynolds, about a football match between prisoners and guards – already remade at least twice.
- ❑ **Escape from Alcatraz (1979)** starring Clint Eastwood: an inmate who's down but not out on the island prison.

and found themselves 'being assaulted on a daily basis' by seasoned convicts. 'They had no leadership,' Corcoran said of the Salinas Valley staff. 'They went through six wardens in three years. They had no senior staff. Is it possible they got a siege mentality? Absolutely. But that was five years ago.' Although he admits that a small proportion of the 49,200 prison staff in California are likely to be bad apples, he says violence and vindictiveness is far from the norm. He feels the 'code of silence' amounts to little more than a natural affinity that develops between guards. 'Without the cameraderie the job would be even more unbearable.'

'My job killed me'

At least one other prison officer in California was hounded after standing up against fellow officers. Doug Pieper witnessed a brief prison riot, the bungled attempt to stop it and the ensuing cover up. Nine months later he put a gun to his head and shot himself, leaving a suicide note that read: 'My job killed me.'

The riot occurred at Folsom Prison on 8 April 2002 when members of the Mexican Mafia and La Nuestra Familia, who had been kept in lockdown for weeks, met in the prison yard. It had been planned for the prisoners to be returned to the yard a few at a time. But a slip up meant they were all released in one go. It also appears that those in the Mexican Mafia advanced menacingly on the others, possibly with concealed weapons.

Watching in horror, Pieper asked if the yard should be shut down. He was told 'Not yet'. During the short battle one prison guard sustained a spinal injury. Although order was quickly restored, Pieper was haunted by what had occurred. His torment was later compounded when he was given a different, inferior job while those he believed to have been at fault were promoted.

In 2000 a prisoner named Zahid Mubarek was killed at Feltham Young Offenders Institute, in the UK, after being put in a cell with known racist, Robert Stewart, who had the letters 'RIP' tattooed on his forehead. After the killing there was speculation in the press that prison officers deliberately placed incompatible cellmates together to spark gladiatorial contests.

> The misery of gaols is not half their evil: they are filled with every corruption which poverty and wickedness can generate between them; with all the shameless and profligate enormities that can be produced by the impudence of ignominy, the rage of want, and the malignity of despair. In a prison, the awe of the publick eye is lost, and the power of the law is spent; there are few fears, there are no blushes. The lewd inflame the lewd, the audacious harden the audacious. Every one fortifies himself as he can against his own sensibility, endeavours to practice on others the arts which are practised on himself; and gains the kindness of his associates by similitude of manners.
>
> Samuel Johnson: *Idler #38* (January 6, 1759)

It was even alleged that officers placed bets on the winner of the fight and the time it took for a fracas to break out. The accusation was largely discounted following an inquiry as no one employed by the prison service furnished investigators with any evidence.

But if the gladiatorial game known as 'Colosseum' was only the product of a rumour mill the practice known as 'wind up' wasn't. In this instance, guards engineered unsuitable cell pairings to provoke a reaction from the inmates serious enough to warrant a disciplinary charge.

Robert Stewart gained notoriety in 2000 when he murdered a fellow prisoner at Feltham Young Offenders Institution in London

PSYCHOLOGICAL WARFARE

So how do the very different tasks of guardianship and punishment get confused in the minds of some prison officers?

In 1971 an experiment by four professors went some way towards explaining this issue. A group of 24 volunteer male students were randomly split into two groups, becoming either prisoners or guards. They moved into Stanford University's Psychology department, which had been mocked up as a prison, to live life strictly by penitentiary rules. Known as the Stanford Prison experiment, it was conducted by Philip Zimbardo, Craig Haney, W. Curtis Banks and David Jaffe.

The guards soon fell into stride, so much so that by the second day the prisoners began to protest at their treatment. The guards, who became increasingly mean, conducted a campaign of harassment against the helpless prisoners and swiftly crushed the rebellion. Even going to the toilet was deemed a privilege that could be withdrawn.

'There were three types of guards,' observed Zimbardo.

> 'First, there were tough but fair guards who followed prison rules. Second, there were "good guys" who did little favors for the prisoners and never punished them. And finally, about a third of the guards were hostile, arbitrary, and inventive in their forms of prisoner humiliation. These guards appeared to thoroughly enjoy the power they wielded, yet none of our preliminary personality tests were able to predict this behavior. The only link between personality and prison behavior was a finding that prisoners with a high degree of authoritarianism endured our authoritarian prison environment longer than did other prisoners.'

As for the prisoners, they responded in various ways but, uniformly, without a sense of unity and purpose. Zimbardo continued:

> 'Prisoners coped with their feelings of frustration and powerlessness in a variety of ways. At first some prisoners rebelled or fought with the guards. Four prisoners reacted by breaking down emotionally as a way to escape the situation. One prisoner developed a psychosomatic rash over his entire body when he learned that his parole request had been turned down. Others tried to cope by being good prisoners, doing everything the guards wanted them to do. One of them [the guards] was even nicknamed 'Sarge' because he was so military-like in executing all commands.'

After five days the study, scheduled to last two weeks, was shelved. Although as equally absorbed in the experiment as the participants, the researchers had been shocked to see the guards escalate their abysmal treatment of the prisoners under cover of darkness, without realising that the 'prison' was being filmed at

Spoons Britain's most notorious killer, Robert Maudsley, is known in the prison service as 'Spoons'. The nickname arose because the body of the paedophile he attacked after being sent to Rampton high security hospital was discovered with the top of his head peeled back and a spoon sticking out of the skull. In the style of Hannibal Lector, it appears Maudsley turned cannibal and ate some of the dead man's brain. In total he has killed four times – on three occasions while in custody – although he insists he is only a risk to those who assault children. He is detained in solitary confinement at Wakefield Prison in a cell measuring 6 ft by 4 ft, with a bullet-proof glass window and a desk and chair made from compressed cardboard. A lover of classical music and poetry, with the IQ of a genius, he has written to *The Times* newspaper asking for a budgerigar for company – which he promises not to eat. Memorably, he has been quoted as saying: 'It does not matter to them whether I am mad or bad. They do not know the answer and they do not care just so long as I am kept out of sight and out of mind.'

all times. It was thought boredom inspired the guards to ever increasing degrees of degrading abuse.

That same day Christina Maslach, a newly qualified PhD, arrived to conduct interviews with the guards and prisoners. When she saw prisoners being marched to the toilet with bags over their heads, chains shackling their legs and gripping the shoulders of the man in front she was horrified. 'It's terrible what you are doing to these boys!' she raged.

'By the end of the study, the prisoners had disintegrated, both as a group and as individuals. There was no longer any group unity; just a bunch of isolated individuals hanging on, much like prisoners of war or hospitalized mental patients. The guards had won total control of the prison, and they commanded the blind obedience of each prisoner,' explained Zimbardo.

> 'We had created an overwhelmingly powerful situation — a situation in which prisoners were withdrawing and behaving in pathological ways, and in which some of the guards were behaving sadistically. Even the "good" guards felt helpless to intervene, and none of the guards quit while the study was in progress.'

The most telling results of the experiment concerned the effects of institutionalization. Young men who were in all other respects ordinary, peace-loving individuals found in themselves a vein of cruelty hitherto unexpected. Of course, the Stanford Prison experiment in no way proved that prison officers as a breed are flawed. Today's rigorous training methods have gone a long way to improving standards.

However, no amount of training of prison officers can prevent the mental deterioration that some prisoners experience when they enter incarceration.

Suicides

There are many prisoners who, like Rodney Hulin, choose to take their own life rather than endure prison existence. Statistically, inmates have higher suicide rates than their community counterparts, according to Suicide and Mental Health Association International (SMHAI). In pre-trial facilities housing short-term inmates, the suicide rate is 10 times that of the outside community. Among sentenced prisoners, the suicide rate is three times higher than in the outside community. For every death that occurs, there are many more suicide attempts.

Stanford psychology professor Philip Zimbardo gives a lecture on Abu Ghraib prison in 2007. He is known for his studies of prison life

It could be because those sent to jail are high suicide risks anyway, being young males, mentally ill or substance abusers.

However, sometimes the psychological impact of arrest and incarceration are simply more than the individual can bear. Most vulnerable people in prison are put on 'suicide watch' so that they can be monitored by staff. Still, deaths occur because staff are simply too stretched or inadequately trained to prevent them. And prisons are not the best places to access community mental health programmes.

The most popular suicide method is hanging. Prisoners may use belts, sheets, shoelaces or items stolen from workshops for the noose. Inmates who have incurred the enmity of a powerful prison gang are also sometimes hanged so that the death looks like suicide. Some prisoners engineer a drugs overdose by squirreling away legitimately distributed medication but most resort to using poisons like cleaners or anti-freeze that they get hold of during the course of prison work. There's also the option of slashing oneself with a sharp object, usually a razor or a fork. One woman prisoner died six days after she swallowed broken glass.

Few, however, choose the brain-pulping route taken by Sawai Palaphol, who killed a two-year-old in Thailand. He collapsed and

TASER is an acronym for Thomas A Swift Electronic Rifle. It is not named after its inventor but after the character in a series of books that first appeared in 1910 and are still being published today. Tom Swift (the A in Taser is gratuitous) is the hero whose technological wizardry drives each plot in the adventure series. The original author was Edward Stratemeyer, but the books now appear under the name of Victor Appleton.

died after repeatedly smashing his head against the cell wall.

PRISON VISITING

While their influence on inmates' lives is undeniable, prison guards can also exert a large amount of control on prison visitors. One woman, Ashe Bandele, told the Commission on Safety and Abuse in America's Prisons about her experiences visiting her husband Rashid in New York jails. There was a dress code that, she said, might suddenly change so that an outfit deemed acceptable one week might be ruled out the next. She was frustrated when guards questioned the kit she took in when accompanied by her baby.

> 'I have argued — and most often lost — about how many bottles I could bring in. (The guard said I could bring two in as I begged my baby will need three, perhaps four, over the course of a six-hour visit.) I have argued — and often lost here, too — about bringing in a change of clothes for my infant who at regular intervals completely soiled her clothes; I never went anywhere else without a back up outfit but at the prison it was viewed as contraband, depending on who was on the door.
>
> 'I have had to fight with guards not to stamp my baby's hand with whatever chemical is in the ink that they mark incoming visitors with. I'd argue: "Are you going to mistake this six-month-old, who puts everything including her hands in her mouth, for a resident of the facility?"'

Bandele, a journalist and author of the book *The Prisoner's Wife*, was subjected to humiliating comments on arriving for visits and found the search of her underwear during conjugal visits particularly galling as bra and thong were elaborately shaken out, usually in front of a group of men. After their daughter was born Rashid was moved between six facilities in a space of five years, making visiting increasingly difficult.

> 'I will never be convinced that [this treatment] made the facility more secure. Indeed, the treatment of family members has the potential to make a facility less secure because it can lead to severe tension between a prisoner and the guard who humiliated or otherwise violated his wife. As a result, I often chose not to tell my husband the many indignities. But how did they change me? I am still discovering that.'

'They have driven my wife mad'

In 2004 a prisoner in Britain revealed his anxieties while he was incarcerated under the Anti-Terrorism, Crime and Security Act, brought in after 9/11. Identified only as Mr 'A', the Algerian national became an al-Qaeda suspect after supplying Chechen fighters with equipment including boots and a sleeping bag. The Act stipulates that, having been judged a risk to the public by the security service MI5, he can be detained without charges.

> 'Just imagine a British man held indefinitely in Algeria,' he

A mother and child wait to be admitted to Camp Diwa in Manila, Philippines, to visit a relative

An inmate receives a visitor at a prison in New Mexico, but is unable to touch her or to talk directly

said. 'This is a slow death and they are destroying my mind.'

Prison conditions were not so bad, he admitted. He has been held at high security Belmarsh Prison, which opened in London in 1991, and Woodhill, near Milton Keynes, Buckinghamshire. 'They look after you, give you a cell on your own. But is it me or my family who is punished? They have driven my wife mad.' Both he and his wife, a European convert to Islam, are suffering from depression. Four of his five children remain traumatized from the dawn raid in December 2001 during which he was arrested. His wife was then eight months pregnant.

He has not seen his teenage daughters for two years and does not like his wife and younger children visiting him in prison.

'Imagine this environment for anyone who has not done any crime. I was scared even to bring [my family] to prison. It will have a great impact seeing all the officers and dogs.'

In one letter they wrote:

'It is unfair for you to be there, and we wish you were here to look after us. We dream about you a lot

and you've been there for too long and we need you here so much.'

Mr A, who insists he is not a terrorist, says his children have told him that almost every night they dream of seeing him coming home. He finds it particularly difficult with his youngest son, born while he was in custody, finding the child's visits with his mother disturbing. 'My son doesn't know me. He screams when he sees me. I can't hold him and can't hug him because he is screaming all the time.'

Despite the risk of torture that looms large in his homeland, he hopes to return to Algeria so that his single abiding wish can be fulfilled: 'Just let me be somewhere with my family'.

'Prison is destructive'

Another prisoner's wife, who wished to remain anonymous, had harsh words for the wide-reaching effects that incarceration wields on innocent families.

'Let's be completely clear about this: most prisoners' families have very little power, status, money or support. The imprisonment of a loved one is not something that people tend to protest about, except in some cases of miscarriages of justice, because the simple truth of the matter is that if you had any power before you were in that situation, it is certainly almost non-existent once you are. You effectively have no rights to privacy in your relationship with your caged family member and getting information, support and your voice heard becomes almost impossible because you are forever worrying that if you object or make too much of a fuss it will simply mean that you don't get a visit or you will be targeted or your loved one will be punished in some way. You become grateful for any crumbs on offer and relieved when, at the new prison, the screws are reasonably pleasant rather than actively hostile.

'Prison is destructive not reformative. How come reformists so rarely acknowledge that prison is mostly about pain and punishment and it brutalizes everyone connected with it? I really don't accept the view that prison staff simply need to be more aware of our problems and the role we play in rehabilitation. Prison has nothing to do with rehabilitation. If it happens at all it happens despite what is being done to prisoners not because of it. If we

Statistics

❑ On 28 November 2003 the prison population in England and Wales stood at 74,182. In the last two years the prison population has increased by nearly 6,000. — *Prison Reform Trust*

❑ The UK has the highest imprisonment rate in the European Union at 139 per 100,000, taking over from Portugal, which has an imprisonment rate of 131 per 100,000. — *Prison Reform Trust*

❑ By the end of the decade Home Office projections predict a prison population anywhere between 91,400 and 109,600. — *UK Home Office*

❑ More than 1,000 inmates were added to US prisons and jails each week from June 2004 to June 2005. — *U.S. Department of Justice*

❑ Two-thirds of the nearly 2.2 million total inmates were in state or federal prisons, and the rest were in local jails. — *US Department of Justice*

❑ Montana's state prison population saw the largest increase in 2004/2005 – 7.9 per cent – closely followed by South Dakota – 7.8 per cent. Both states have reported a spike in methamphetamine addiction, particularly among female prisoners. — *US Department of Justice*

❑ At mid-year 2005, nearly 60 per cent of offenders in local jails were racial or ethnic minorities, a statistic that has not changed in the past decade. — *US Department of Justice*

❑ At mid-year 2005, nearly 4.7 per cent of black men, nearly 2 per cent of Hispanic men, and 0.7 per cent of white men nationwide were in a prison or jail. — *US Department of Justice*

❑ Women represent about 13 per cent of the US jail population, a 2.5 per cent increase over the past decade. — *US Department of Justice*

are the single biggest factor in determining re-offending rates then how come we are treated, for the most part, like dirt?'

However, not all relatives of inmates have been willing to succumb to bleak notions of helplessness. Perhaps this is due to the extraordinary hopelessness of their situation. Possibly they feel they have nothing left to lose. But the mothers of those arrested by the authorities in Argentina during seven shocking years of the 'Dirty War' banded together to form a remarkable and persistent political force that continued for more than 20 years.

Dirty War

When a military junta took control of Argentina in 1976, the generals who took command claimed they would stem a tide of domestic terrorism that had brought chaos to the capital Buenos Aires and beyond. Ultimately, that meant arrest, torture and even death for anyone perceived to have leftist tendencies. The victims were snatched from the streets by the police or army units and became known as the 'desaparecidos', the 'disappeared'.

Although a climate of fear cloaked the country, some mothers were determined to discover the fate of their children after they had been taken. At first the women went individually to detention centres, police stations and government offices, achieving little. Then they grouped together and decided to demonstrate at a site best known as a memorial of Argentina's independence from Spain. They gathered at the same spot every Thursday bearing pictures of the missing and became known as the Mothers of the Plaza de Mayo, notable for their white headscarves and an encompassing grief known only to parents whose offspring had suffered an untimely death.

It wasn't always easy. One of the founders of the Mothers of the Plaza de Mayo, Azucena Villaflor, was herself kidnapped, tortured and killed by the regime. It was only in 2005 that her family discovered exactly what had happened to her.

She had been kept in the torture cells of the Navy Mechanics School, known as ESMA, before being bundled aboard a military aircraft and thrown out. Her body was washed up on a beach and only identified much later through DNA testing.

Nursing mothers had newborn babies ripped from their arms before being killed. An estimated 500 children then became adoptees for childless couples associated with the military. Even when the junta gave way to democracy in 1983 the demonstrating mothers continued their weekly parade.

The interior of the detention centre at Rosario, Argentina, now a memorial to those who disappeared during the military dictatorship

Nilda Eloy was among those arrested during Argentina's 'Dirty War'. She was taken from her parents' home one night on the flimsy pretext that she once had a boyfriend with left-wing links.

'You were never sure when you went to work that you'd get home that night. The cops or soldiers would pull passengers off a bus and brutalize half of them on the off chance that somebody might have left-wing connections. Just one name in an address book could set off a chain of arrests and, as I learnt, once inside the machinery of repression you were quickly reduced to little better than a thing, an object.'

She was tortured with an electric cattle prod, suffocated with a plastic bag until she blacked out in a process known as 'dry drowning', starved, deprived of water, beaten and kept hooded or blindfolded. She was released after three years in captivity and discovered that her parents had mounted a vigil outside the federal prison where she had been held. Twenty years later she heard the unmistakable voice of her chief tormentor, a police interrogator, Miguel Etchecolatz, during a television interview and contacted human rights groups that were pressing for his re-trial. Today she claims: 'The ghosts of the dirty war are still among us'.

The sheer persistence of the Mothers of the Plaza de Mayo has kept the atrocities very much in the public eye. Although it is not known exactly how many people died during the 'Dirty War' at the hands of torturers and murderers working for the right-wing regime, estimates range between 9,000 and 30,000. In all probability, the truth will never be known for certain. Records were destroyed and those who know are keeping silent.

A demonstration by the Mothers of the Plaza de Mayo in Buenos Aires

New trials

It wasn't only Argentinians who were killed. The victims included French nuns, a Swedish teenager and a group of Italians with dual citizenship. However, attempts to bring to justice those responsible for the abductions and deaths were thwarted by an amnesty introduced following pressure from the military. Only now, more than 20 years after the killings, are trials of the accused taking place. Even so, the controversy took a new twist following the disappearance in September 2006 of a key witness, Jorge Julio

Lopez, who had given evidence against Miguel Etchecolatz.

Years before, through a crack in his cell door, Lopez had seen a married couple from his neighbourhood shot dead by Etchecolatz. The verdict was not in doubt. Etchecolatz had already been jailed – and freed – for human-

Although it is not known exactly how many people died during the 'Dirty War', estimates range between 9,000 and 30,000

rights violations and had stated unequivocally at his trial that he had no regrets about liquidating 'enemies of the state'. He was sent to jail for life.

But before Etcheclotz was sentenced a second time, Lopez, 77, had vanished. His name was soon added to the list of desaparecidos, more than 30 years after it was deemed complete.

Only the present government's pledge to root out and jail the killers of their husbands, sons and daughters has made the Mothers end their weekly parade. Yet their campaign to keep the issue of the desaparecidos in the public eye, when plenty of people wanted it swept under the carpet, ultimately helped bring sadistic and murderous men to justice. ESMA, the death camp where as many as 5,000 were killed is being turned into a museum of remembrance.

Prison Speak

For anyone finding themselves behind bars in the UK, this is a translation guide for the words they could expect to hear:

- ❑ **Chip net:** safety net strung between prison landings
- ❑ **Jimmy** or **Jimmy Boyle:** foil used for smoking heroin
- ❑ **Pie and liquor:** vicar
- ❑ **Pad:** cell
- ❑ **Pad spin:** cell search
- ❑ **Kanga** or **The Man:** prison guard
- ❑ **Burglars:** prison security responsible for cell searches
- ❑ **Ghosting:** being transferred to another prison without notice
- ❑ **Wet up** or **Jug up:** scalding someone with boiling water
- ❑ **Apple** or **Apple Core:** score, either twenty years or twenty pounds
- ❑ **Salmon and trout:** snout or tobacco
- ❑ **Diesel:** prison tea
- ❑ **Shit and a shave:** short sentence

4 BREAKING UP & BREAKING OUT

Two issues continually bubble under the surface in prisons. They don't occur often but riots and escapes are the life blood of prison folklore. When they do happen they don't cause ripples, they cause tidal waves.

Riots are usually in direct response to poor living conditions. Prisoners tend to be a disparate bunch but they can be united, at least for a few short hours, if they are deprived of food or other basic necessities. There is, however, also a chance that a riot will happen when inmates are bored and seeking an outlet for their pent-up energies. Wardens are trained to spot the symptoms of an impending blow-up.

Escapes are central to the psyche of some inmates although the vast majority has little interest in risking fresh and weighty sentences if breakouts go awry. Some people on the outside see an escapee as a glamorous fugitive, pitting his wits, like a cunning fox, against lawmen. In reality he's more likely to be a mean and dangerous dog, ready to savage anyone who stands in his way.

Rioting prisoners at Attica State Prison, New York, raise their fists to show solidarity in October 1971

IN 1971 a volatile political atmosphere infected an overcrowded New York prison, with deadly consequences. Anti-war sentiment was at fever pitch as America's involvement in Vietnam dragged on. It had been heightened the previous year when the National Guard had opened fire on unarmed student protestors.

America's Civil Rights Act was only seven years old and symptoms of racism were still keenly felt. Although more than half the inmates inside Attica Prison were black, all the prison officers were white and some were openly racist. When the black population of Attica heard about the death that year of icon George Jackson at the hands of a white prison officer tensions soared. However, there was no evidence that a riot was imminent.

Aside from the political stirrings, conditions inside the prison were poor. Men were given two buckets in their cells, one for food, the other to use as a toilet. But after they were emptied there was no way of telling which was which. The inmate population stood at an estimated 2,200 – about 1,000 more than the prison was intended to house.

A considerable number of the white prisoners were subjected to the same deplorable squalor, including anti-capitalist protestor, Sam Melville. Nonetheless, the man who bombed New York's financial district was settling in well in prison. In a letter to a friend written before the riot he concluded: 'I think the combination of age and the greater coming together is responsible for the speed of the passing time. It's six months now and I can tell you truthfully few periods in my life have passed so quickly. I am in excellent physical and emotional health. There are doubtless subtle surprises ahead but I feel secure and ready.'

Before the infamous riot had ended Melville lay dead from gunshot wounds to the head.

Requests denied

It began on 9 September 1971 after a prisoner was locked in his cell while fellow inmates went to breakfast. When the rumour circulated that he was going to be tortured, five inmates freed him. Shortly after that violence erupted and prison officer William Quinn, 28, was allegedly tossed out of a window, dying two days later from his injuries. Three inmates were also killed by the rioters. Prisoners armed with pipes, chains and baseball bats took 42 hostages and occupied one wing of the prison.

'If we can't live as men we sure as hell can die as men,' said one of the rioters. Still, they catered thoughtfully for their hostages, became well-organized and entered into negotiations.

For their part, the authorities were willing to concede negotiating points to the prisoners. However, they refused to grant an amnesty to those involved. The somewhat optimistic request by the prisoners to be taken to a 'non-Imperialistic' country was also denied.

After four days New York governor, Nelson Rockefeller, decided to break the palpable tension at the prison by sending in armed troops. On a damp Monday morning helicopters fired tear gas into the yard controlled by the prisoners. Then law enforcement officers fired 2,000 rounds in six minutes, killing 29 prisoners and 10 hostages. Claims made to the media that prisoners had slit the throats of the hostages proved to be totally false.

It has often been called the bloodiest one-day encounter between Americans since the Civil War. Ironically, while libertarians believed vile conditions were the cause of the unrest, local people thought the permissive regime at the prison was to blame. When prison officers reclaimed the jail, the subsequent punishment of inmates involved in the riot was merciless.

The harsh post-riot treatment was the basis of a law suit filed by inmates and victims' families and in 2004 the respective lawyers agreed a $12 million settlement.

SANTA FE

DRUNK ON HOOCH

While events at Attica were marked by solidarity among prisoners, the riot that took place nine years later in Santa Fe is remembered more for its appalling savagery.

And this time it wasn't a case of armed guards lashing out at inmates. In the New Mexico penitentiary prisoners turned on one another with merciless barbarity.

The trouble began in the early hours of 2 February 1980 when two guards came across a couple of inmates drunk on home-made hooch. Perhaps fuelled by the alcohol, the men overpowered the guards, ran from the scene and dashed into a nearby control centre. The guard in charge fled, leaving a set of keys. With these the prisoners could release the other inmates at will.

Informers who had been fostered by the prison authorities were kept in separate quarters for their own protection. Now, outraged inmates sought out the so-called snitches to exact revenge. If they couldn't find the right keys to open the doors, the rampaging men used a blow torch to burn a route to their terrified quarry.

'There's blood all over this goddam corridor'

One man was found hanged with the word 'rat' carved into his chest. Another was discovered with an iron bar run through his skull from ear to ear. Law enforcement officers gathering at

A National Guardsman keeps a wary watch on prisoners in the aftermath of a riot at the New Mexico State Prison. The inmates wrapped themselves in blankets to stave off the cold

the perimeter watched in horror as prisoners murdered a man by blow torch. 33 inmates were killed, their corpses dismembered and burnt. One man was decapitated.

As the torture and killing unfolded the authorities decided against intervention in the hope of saving the lives of the 10 guards being held hostages inside. Remarkably, although beaten, stabbed and sodomized, none were murdered. Two guards and a medical technician, who were hidden by inmates during the violence, remained undiscovered.

One man was discovered with an iron bar run through his skull from ear to ear

However, it was starkly obvious that violence on a major scale had been unleashed inside. An ominous message came through on a two-way radio. 'Attention, attention, all units. You stop killing each other. There's blood all over this goddam corridor.'

In addition, the rioters attacked the very fabric of the prison, built in 1956. They battered holes through six-inch re-inforced concrete, burned down steel doors and smashed furniture to matchsticks. They also emptied the shelves of the pharmacy of drugs. Some broke into workshops to sniff glue.

Eventually, though, the perpetrators came down from their variously-induced highs and began to give themselves up to the patiently waiting state troopers standing by the 15 ft fences. They joined scores of other prisoners gathering there, putting themselves out of harm's way.

Ghost figures from a nether world

Secretary of Corrections, Adolph Saenz, described the scene like this:

> 'To the north of the city of Santa Fe, the sun crested the snow-covered Sangre de Cristo Mountains. Below the highlands, on the desert plateau, dark smoke from the burning penal institution spiraled upward in the windless sky. National Guard troops and State Police surrounded the penitentiary. They stood immobile, twenty to thirty yards apart, outside the barbed wire fence encircling the prison,

watching for signs of escape. During the night, approximately two hundred inmates had managed to flee the violence inside the prison walls, seeking refuge in the prison yard.

'Injured inmates, some with mutilations, wandered aimlessly in the smoke-filled courtyard. Outside the perimeter fence, prison officials watched and waited...'

There seemed little cohesion among the rioters, about a dozen of whom were thought to have been responsible for the killings.

The 1990 riot at Strangeways Prison in Manchester was the most violent and expensive in British history

Eventually a list of 11 basic demands was issued, one being the attendance of journalists at the scene. In return some of the hostages were released.

One of the first journalists to arrive was Steve Northup of *Time* magazine. 'There was smoke everywhere. You could see people giving themselves up — ghostlike figures coming out, waving white sheets. It was a nether world.'

After 36 hours the troopers moved in and regained control of the prison without firing a shot. Ninety prisoners needed hospital treatment, many for the effects of drug overdoses. Overcrowding, unsanitary conditions and lax security probably contributed to the catastrophe. Race does not appear to have played a part. It may well have been that having so many vicious men locked in one place lead to the rage that engulfed the jail. In any event, prisoners were dispersed among several jails in case bad chemistry between inmates had played its part.

Although the penitentiary was partially refurbished, it was finally closed in 1997.

GREAT BRITAIN

STRANGEWAYS RIOT

In Britain, the worst prison riot wasn't coloured with blood; it earned notoriety because of its longevity, lasting no fewer than 25 days.

Nobody died in the unrest at Strangeways Prison, in Manchester, although 200 inmates and staff were injured. The damage inflicted on the Victorian building cost about £100 million to repair.

Trouble started on 1 April 1990 – All Fools Day – following a sermon in the prison chapel. There was a healthy congregation that morning of about 300 – implying that the action was planned. A prisoner, later identified as Paul Taylor, stood up and said: 'This man has just talked about the blessing of the heart and how a hardened heart can be delivered. No it cannot, not with resentment, anger and bitterness and hatred being instilled in people.'

Prison officers beat a hasty retreat – but not before a prisoner had taken a set of keys, which meant other inmates could be released with ease.

Masked prisoners soon made their way to the chapel roof where they hurled slate tiles at the police and prison officers gathering below. 'Stop the brutality. We are not taking it any more,' one bellowed through a loudspeaker. 'We are up here because we have had enough of being treated like s**t. We're not animals. We are human beings.'

Rioters set fire to the gym, chapel and some cells. Early reports that rioters had forced their way into E-wing, where sex offenders were held in isolation, and killed 12 later proved to be wrong.

One prisoner was 17-year-old Jason Ogden, who later recalled the terror he felt:

'It was horrific. I just wanted a way out. One bloke handed me a meat cleaver and I just took it because I didn't want to look like I wasn't doing anything. I just threw it down when I got round the corner.

'I saw people slashed, and the place was six inches deep in water because the toilet block was smashed up. One lad was on protection on the landing above us, but he wasn't a sex offender, he just wouldn't take the sentence for his co-accused. Lads were making their way up there carrying sticks and shouting. I never saw him again.'

Slopping out

While prison officials tried to evacuate as many prisoners as possible the ring-leaders climbed on to the roof every evening to entertain local people and the assembled media. It wasn't until 25 April that the last five surrendered peacefully.

Afterwards the harsh conditions within the prison, built in 1869 and barely modernized, became known. Up to three prisoners were sharing single cells and they had to 'slop out' each day (empty a bucket of urine and faeces) because they had no access to a toilet. As a result of the riot, slopping out was ended and authorities pledged to improve conditions in Britain's many Victorian jails.

The imposing walls of Fremantle Prison, Western Australia, now a popular tourist attraction

AUSTRALIA

RIOT AND ESCAPE

On 4 January 1988 a prison in Fremantle, Western Australia, was partially destroyed in a riot that began when two prisoners delivering tea threw 50 litres of boiling water from the urns at guards. In the mayhem that followed, 70 prisoners from the wing housing the prison's most violent inmates rushed the gates, forcing them open. They then lit a fire, fuelling it with furniture ripped from cells opened with stolen keys.

The fire turned into an inferno and the prison roof collapsed. Firemen arriving on the scene discovered that the prison gates, built by convict labour more than 100 years before, were too narrow for the fire engines to get through. It took 19 hours before the fire was brought under control, by which time damage valued at Aus $1.8 million had been caused.

In fact, it was not the riot but a later escape attempt that got out of hand which became the big story. The brains behind the bid was

Brenden Abbott, a notorious bank robber who had collected the petrol used to spark the original blaze from the prison lawnmowers. Evidently, he was not enjoying incarceration at Fremantle. As he later recalled: 'Fremantle was a right shithole. I remember one night waking up because of a cockroach having a feed from my mouth'.

Unable to make good his escape in the chaos that day he waited a year before breaking out of Fremantle. On the run for nearly six years, Abbott was eventually recaptured in 1995 yet escaped from the Sir David Longland Prison in Queensland two years afterwards. (Although Fremantle was rebuilt following the fire it was closed

The island prison of Alcatraz stands in San Francisco Bay, close to the famous Golden Gate Bridge

soon afterwards and today it is a popular tourist attraction.)

Postcard bandit

A career bank robber, Abbott continued to pursue his trade, to the frustration of police. To the public he was the Postcard Bandit, taunting police by sending then postcards of his travels. In fact, these stories were invented. It was true, though, that police recovered photographs of Abbott at the scene of his crimes showing officers at work over the robber's shoulder.

He was finally captured again in 1998 and kept in solitary confinement for five years, the longest detention of this type given to any Australian inmate; a reflection, perhaps, of his capacity to embarrass the authorities. His release date is 2020, and he will still have charges to face in two other Australian states.

USA

ALCATRAZ

As long as there are prisons there will be jail breaks; some prisoners like Abbott seem to have the need to flee written into their DNA. For these inmates there are prisons like Alcatraz. Perched on an island in the swirling currents of San Francisco Bay, it became a federal jail in 1934, during the heyday of organized crime in America's big cities. It was the destination for 300 of the system's most hardened inmates, each occupying a single cell sited by a perimeter wall to reduce the opportunity for escape.

Alcatraz was not only a suitable holding pen for notorious offenders, it was a chilling symbol of an impenetrable penitentiary, visible from the city. It had its fair share of infamous inmates including Al Capone and Robert 'Birdman' Stroud, a murderer who earned his ornithological reputation at a previous prison and was not permitted to keep birds on the island.

Escape from Alcatraz

But the prison is probably best remembered for escape attempts, none of which are

Burt Lancaster starred in the movie *The Bird Man of Alcatraz*, which was based on true events in the notorious prison

believed to have been successful. There were 14 different breakouts involving 36 inmates, two of whom tried to escape twice. Seven were shot and killed in the process, twenty-three were recaptured and three drowned. Five men from two different escape bids are unaccounted for but are widely thought to have disappeared into the dark waters of the bay.

In 1945 an inmate who worked on the prison docks loading clothes made by inmates stole, over the course of several months, individual items until he had assembled an entire military uniform. One day he hid the clothes by the dock, put them on while the guards were distracted and leapt aboard a departing boat. Unfortunately for him, his absence was noticed immediately and the prison radioed the ship to return, thus ending the convict's brief spell of liberty.

Another man, in 1962, fared little better. He had loosened and removed a bar across a storage room window and covered himself with lard to slither through the small gap. He survived the bay's dangerous currents and beached himself near the Golden Gate Bridge. But he was so tired from his exploits that he fell asleep and was recaptured before leaving the shore.

An attempt at a mass jail break in 1946 resulted in a shoot out between prisoners and prison officers. Alcatraz warden James A Johnston was so alarmed that he called in the Marines, Coast Guard and Navy to help contain the situation. The prison officers soon won back the cell block where some of their colleagues had been taken hostage, though not before two of these were killed. Three of the inmates were killed and two were sent to the gas chamber at San Quentin for their role in the mutiny. Another was sentenced to 99 years.

Perhaps the best-remembered escape also took place in 1962, when four men broke out by surreptitiously drilling holes into a utility corridor behind their cells. To prevent their absence from being immediately detected, they left hand-made heads in their beds. Earlier they had hidden a hastily-constructed raft at the water's edge with which to cross the treacherous straits to freedom.

In the end, one man was left behind because the hole he had dug was not large enough to squeeze through. The fate of Frank Morris and the brothers John and Clarence Anglin is, however, unknown. There was at least one report from a ship in the area of seeing a body in the water soon after the break out, though no conclusive evidence ever emerged about whether the men drowned in their desperate bid to escape from Alcatraz or lived thereafter incognito, having pulled off an extraordinary feat.

The Hole

Why were prisoners so keen to leave Alcatraz? Well, to begin with, the daily schedule was harsh, beginning at 6.30 am and involving plenty of hard labour. Also, all privileges, including visits, had to be earned. Then there was the highly-regimented existence, with its 12 head counts a day, and transgressors very often found themselves in 'The Hole', a row of solitary cells with sink, toilet and a single low-wattage bulb. Perpetual offenders were sent to the dreaded 'strip cell', a dark, steel-encased tomb-like place without lights or a sink. The toilet was a hole in the ground. Prisoners dispatched there were forced to remain naked day and night. Only at night were they permitted a mattress for the concrete bed. Fortunately for the prisoners, confinement in the strip cell usually lasted only a few days.

However, the real reason that so many men yearned to leave Alcatraz was the policy of silence instituted by Warden Johnston. Its effects were so disturbing that one prisoner, convicted gangster Rufe Persful, cut off his fingers with a hatchet while in a workshop to get away from the aching isolation it created. Yet even when the silence rule was relaxed, life in Alcatraz was tough.

By the 1950s life behind bars on the island had eased and Alcatraz came to resemble almost every other American prison – except for the cost of running it. The prison finally closed in 1964 when the last prisoner, Alf Banks, was shipped out. It now attracts a million tourists a year.

'A private purgatory where carefully chosen victims are slowly driven mad.' — **An Alcatraz inmate comments on 'the Hole'**

Rikers Island

ISLAND PRISONS

❑ **ROBBEN ISLAND, Cape Town, South Africa (right).** A significant prison during the Apartheid era, among its inmates were Nelson Mandela (far right, with ex-US president Bill Clinton) and other prominent members of the African National Congress after they campaigned for equal rights. Formerly a leper colony, it opened as a prison in 1960. Working in the chalk mines was part of the punishment regime.

❑ **ST HELENA, mouth of the Brisbane River, Queensland, Australia.** An island prison between 1867 and 1932. With swift tides, rip currents and man-eating sharks, the waters around the island were a better barrier to escape than walls. Only one man fled the jail, in 1924, and Charles Leslie only succeeded because he had accomplices waiting offshore with a boat.

❑ **NORFOLK ISLAND, 1,250 miles northwest of Sydney, Australia.** Twice a Pacific penal colony in the nineteenth century, it was notorious for the cruelty and sadism of its commandants and the suffering of its convict residents who were regularly lashed and kept short of food. However, after the prison closed the island was settled in 1856 and remained remarkably crime-free until the murder of 29-year-old Janelle Patton in 2002. Glenn McNeill, a chef from New Zealand, was convicted of her murder in 2007.

❑ **RIKERS ISLAND, New York City (top).** Just miles from the Statue of Liberty, it lies off the coast of Manhattan in the East River and houses some 15,000 inmates in nine male and one female prison blocks. Known to its residents as 'the Rock', it has been a prison since the island was sold to the city in 1884. A picture of the crucifixion in red and black ink by Salvador Dali used to grace its walls. In 2003 the valuable picture was replaced by a replica. Three prison guards were prosecuted for the theft but the original has not yet been recovered.

The chalk mines on Robben Island

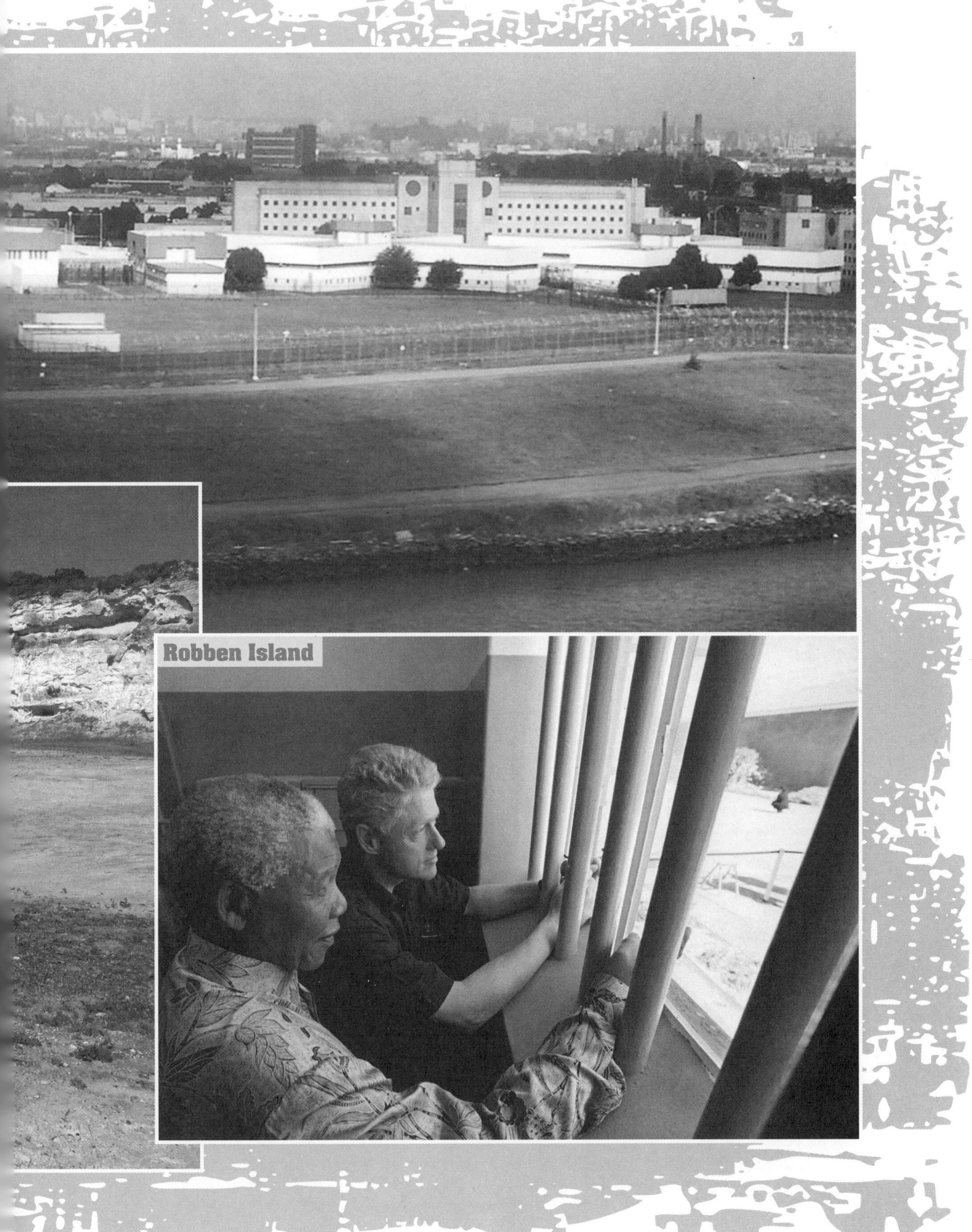
Robben Island

DEVIL'S ISLAND, FRENCH GUIANA

LIBERATING FRANCE

The infamous Devil's Island, set up under Napoleon III

Still, Alcatraz was by no means as notorious as Devil's Island, perhaps the international benchmark in appalling prisons. The name is misleading. Devil's Island was one of three islands that, together with a sizeable slice of mainland French Guiana, comprised the penal colony opened in 1852 by Napoleon III. It operated for nearly a century, during which time thousands of hardcore and novice criminals were sent there from mainland France. The aim was clear: to rid mother France of trouble-makers and dissenters. The technique was brutally effective.

Forty per cent of new arrivals to the colony died within the first year. Of the 80,000 or so who were transported there during the colony's 94-year existence, few made it back to France. Vulnerable to the effects of tropical diseases and exhaustion, prisoners existed in a state of perpetual terror, not knowing if the fierce guards or unfamiliar environment would deal them a deadly blow.

NORMAN PARKER, a convicted murderer turned successful author who spent more than 20 years in prison, explains why riots happen: 'Cutbacks in expenditure have led to reductions in workshops and associations and mean people often spend 23 hours a day locked up. That is what cracks people up.'

Shackled prisoners worked 12 hours a day in the sun and oppressive heat and faced perils as diverse as poisonous snakes and malaria-carrying mosquitoes. They survived on starvation rations.

Road to nowhere

Many men worked and died waist-deep in water in the timber camps, where they were forced to meet an arduous daily quota or suffer dire punishment. The most deadly camp was at Kourou, where convicts were made to build a road – Route Zero – though many suffered from the twin plagues of disease and hunger. So few survived that the road never stretched beyond 25 kilometres. Solitary confinement, another commonly employed punishment, was a roofless, subterranean cell on the island of St Joseph, known among inmates as the 'devourer of men'. Armed guards peering in as they paced its boundaries, saw crouching, cowed prisoners staring back.

For those guilty of minor infringements the shadow of the guillotine still loomed large. The unforgiving blade was France's chosen method of delivering capital punishment and was in regular use. Victim's heads were preserved in alcohol and sent back to France as proof that justice had been done.

Devil's Island was often earmarked for political prisoners. It became famous for one of its inhabitants, Alfred Dreyfus, a French army officer wrongly accused of spying in a case that dragged on for years. Dreyfus and his supporters eventually unveiled corruption and anti-semitism among the top brass as well as unmasking the true traitor, a Major Esterhazy.

Those fortunate enough to survive their sentences, which usually amounted to a minimum of eight years, were then obliged to spend a similar length of time in French Guiana as authorities in France tried to financially improve the colony.

Escaping the devil's clutches

There were only three ways of fleeing the purgatory of forced labour in French Guiana: by sea, by crossing into Dutch Guiana or by hacking a path through virgin jungle into neighbouring Brazil.

Those who chose the sea had to contend with strong currents and shark-infested waters.

Anyone heading for Dutch Guiana probably went via dugout canoe and risked ending up as food for the ravenous piranha fish that patrolled the River Maroni. Convicts choosing to travel by land were likely to have their bones picked clean by giant, marauding ants. Even if they survived the mortal threats posed by natural predators, convicts had to avoid the merciless bounty hunters who roamed the region, eager to cash in on the reward offered for escapees. And prisoners were always sent back if they were captured by guards of the Dutch colony, who were weary of convict excesses.

Perhaps the most famous inmate of Devil's Island was Alfred Dreyfus, a French army officer wrongly convicted of espionages

To enter Brazil meant almost certain death from encounters with any number of fierce or poisonous jungle creatures lurking beneath the rainforest canopy.

Of course any choice of escape was accompanied a real threat of disease.

In addition to Dreyfus, two other men brought to note the atrocious conditions that weighed on inmates.

One was Rene Belbenoit (1899-1959) who was sent to Devil's Island in 1920 after stealing pearls from the Countess of Entre-meuse, in Paris. As prisoner number 46635, he tried to

escape four times, on one occasion helping to butcher a fellow escapee who turned murderer. For these breakouts he earned 50 months in solitary confinement.

At this time he provided material for author Blair Niles, who would write two books exposing the horrors at Devil's Island based on a manuscript written by Belbenoit. Only when he had completed his sentence in 1934 and was working in French Guiana as a 'compulsory volunteer' did he make good his escape using a dugout canoe.

As he paddled to freedom he reflected that only 15 men, including himself, of the 700 sent across the Atlantic with him 17 years before had survived.

He worked his way up the South American coast, aided by the British in Trinidad, and survived a close shave with French authorities keen to return him once more to Devil's Island.

Belbenoit financed his adventure through South America through the sale of exotic butterflies that he captured in the jungle with a long-handled net. Despite the deprivations of his fugitive life, he continually wrote in his journal.

Eight inmates of Devil's Island who escaped in August 1940 as the prison regime fell into chaos following the surrender of France to Germany during the Second World War

Dustin Hoffman in his role as a prisoner on Devil's Island for the movie *Papillon*.

'I have read of the harrowing adventures of men who went into South American jungles well provisioned and armed and with guides. I smile, because I left Cartagena with nothing, not even a pocket knife, and lived in the jungle for almost six months. Five or six big jaguars that I encountered looked at me curiously and then scampered off. They were well fed on deer and pigs, and apparently had no wish to taste a half-starved Frenchman. At first the snakes bothered me, but finally I became accustomed to them... When this is published, I hope I shall be safely in the jungles again and free. I say I am free, but actually I am not free, for I am a Frenchman, and I can never return to France.'

He published a book, *Dry Guillotine*, in 1938 after reaching America, which ultimately became his home. He spent the rest of his life attacking the inequities of the French justice system.

In 1999 librarian Lucy Dudko armed herself with a gun and hijacked a helicopter during a 'joyride' over Sydney, Australia. She ordered the pilot to land on Silverwater Jail's sports ground, scooped up her prisoner lover and flew off amid a hail of cheers from inmates and bullets from prison officers.

After they landed in a nearby park they hijacked a taxi to complete their escape. Following six weeks on the run, Dudko and convicted armed robber John Killick were finally captured in a tourist park. Dudko served seven years of a ten-year sentence for helping Killick escape from the maximum security unit, assaulting the helicopter pilot, taking and holding the taxi driver for advantage, and possessing a gun. Killick will not be freed from his 23-year sentence until 2013.

Butterfly mind

Perhaps even more famous was Frenchman Henri Charriere (1906-73), better known as 'Papillon' – The Butterfly.

He was arrested in 1931, framed, he insisted, for the murder of a pimp, and dispatched to the South American penal colony. An escape attempt in 1933 resulted in a year of liberty until he was recaptured in Colombia. Another time he tried to flee by feigning mental illness. On one occasion his bid to escape was foiled by an informer. After killing the snitch he was saddled with still more time in penal servitude.

Finally, he asked to be sent to Devil's Island itself, thought to be escape-proof. The authorities, obviously, were delighted to comply with the request. There, Charriere formulated the most basic of his flight plans: a sack of coconuts upon which he would float to freedom. He persuaded another prisoner to join him in the enterprise. Hours spent studying the currents and wave patterns paid off. Three days and nights after launching from Devil's Island, he and his colleague drew close to the mainland. Keen to make land, his friend slipped off the raft prematurely and was sucked to his death in quicksand. Charriere stayed aboard until he was safely nudging solid ground. He eventually made it to Venezuela where he became a citizen and produced his book *Papillon*, named after the butterfly tattoo on his chest.

Doubt still remains about the veracity of his story. Rumours abound that Papillon did not die, as reported, of throat cancer in 1973 but may be alive even today.

Adding to the sense of mystery surrounding the entire story is the recent claim by Charles Brunier, a 104-year-old resident of an old people's home in Paris with a butterfly tattoo, that the story published by Charriere is his own. Official records show that both men were in the 'bagne', as Devil's Island is known in France, but can substantiate little else about the claim.

The last of the colony's inmates were repatriated to France in 1952 as Devil's Island at last fell victim to its outrageously high running costs and a concerted campaign by the French Salvation Army to halt the brutal punishments. Like many other places marked by the depths of human misery it has become a tourist attraction.

The daring 1986 escape by helicopter from a French prison by Michel Vaujour has entered prison folklore

FRANCE

HELICOPTER HEIST

Even today, French prisons are infamously vile places. This might go some way towards explaining the extraordinary lengths to which some prisoners have gone to in order to escape.

For two years diminutive brunette, Lena Rigon, was a model pupil during helicopter flying lessons. A single mother of two, she impressed instructors with her dedication and they were delighted when she qualified as a pilot.

The next time she was seen at the controls of a helicopter, on 2 May 1986, she was hovering over the roof of La Sante Prison in Paris. When she eventually flew off, a prisoner was clinging to a helicopter skid. Minutes later they landed at a nearby soccer pitch and fled in a waiting car.

Her name wasn't in fact Lena Rigon, but Nadine Vaujour, whose husband Michel was serving 28 years for attempted murder and armed robbery. This was his fourth – and most spectacular – escape from incarceration.

On this occasion he used a fake pistol and nectarines painted to look like grenades to get past guards and onto the prison roof. In 1979 he had sculpted a gun from soap and used it to threaten guards and flee from jail.

However, his freedom was short-lived. That same year he was one of three wig-wearing robbers involved in a bungled bank raid. Vaujour took a shot to the head from a .357 Magnum, which put him in a coma for weeks. Police identified him through fingerprints and tattoos.

Nadine, meanwhile, had been arrested at a villa in southwestern France just before the raid after she was recognized by a policeman in the area.

Vaujour was in no fit state to plot another escape. Formerly France's Public Enemy Number One, he now had difficulty communicating with others. A jailed policeman who befriended him taught him to speak again and a yoga course beckoned him towards an inner calm.

He was finally released from prison in September 2003, aged 52, having spent just 40 months of his adult life as a free man.

Later Vaujour admitted that the helicopter escape was like 'an enormous kick, a flame of adrenalin with no limits'. His book about his career, *My Most Beautiful Escape*, became a bestseller.

The man of 1,000 faces

Around the same time, another Frenchman, Jacques Mesnes, also became famous as an audacious escape artist. In 1978 he became one of the first people to flee La Santé Prison in Paris, enraging French authorities. The following year he died in his car, cut down by a hail of bullets fired by the French police. His death bore all the hallmarks of an execution and was still being investigated by the government 25 years later.

Born in Clichy in 1936, Mesnes was twice expelled from school before joining the army. The small efforts he made to 'go straight' following his first arrest in 1962 were thwarted by his love of fine wines, good food, designer clothes and fast cars.

The first daring jail break he planned actually took place in Canada. Using stolen pliers, he and fellow inmates cut through three fences and crawled to freedom. The escape was so simple that he and an accomplice planned to return the following week to release all 56 inmates on the maximum security wing. Although he gathered sufficient weapons and getaway cars for the exploit the presence of police and prison guards, significantly increased since his disappearance, put paid to the scheme.

By 1973 he was back in France and aware that his activities could soon land him back in court. So he planned his escape even before his arrest. As a free man he visited the Palais de Justice in Compiegne, on the outskirts of Paris, to hatch a plan that he passed on to colleagues.

Just as he suspected, he was arrested and dispatched to the courthouse at Compiegne. On the way he joked with a police officer that he would be out in three months. The officer laughed, thinking Mesnes was destined for the impenetrable fortress of La Sante. Feigning a stomach ailment, Mesnes found a gun in a toilet cistern just as he had marked on his blueprint and, using a judge as a human shield, made his way to the getaway vehicle.

Not only was he France's most wanted man, Mesnes was also a master of disguise, earning the nickname 'the man with 1,000 faces'. He was only re-captured, in 1973, because he was betrayed by a member of his own gang.

This time, as police edged towards his flat, he kept them in negotiations while he destroyed incriminating evidence. When he opened the door the paperwork was reduced to ashes – he offered the police commissioner champagne to mark the occasion.

He was sent straight to La Sante. He thought he could escape from the courtroom during his trial, but the investigation into his case dragged on, with no court date in sight. Mesnes knew that if he wanted to be free again he would have to break out of La Sante – the first person to accomplish such a feat.

As he pored over escape plans, he wrote his biography, *L'Instinct de Mort* (The Killing Instinct). In it he boasted of committing murders, which altered the public perception of him being a stylish 'Robin Hood'. Unable to pull off an escape during his court hearing in 1977, he waited until the following year when he held up guards, stole their uniforms and used workmen's ladders to scale the maximum security wing of the prison. Eight days later he was back in business, committing two armed robberies on the same day.

Eventually the police tracked him down and shot him dead. There's speculation that his death was ordered by French authorities who were embarrassed and angered by his boldness. At the scene of the shootout, however, police saw him lean across to the glove compartment of his car after his route had been blocked. Later, weapons were found inside the car. Associates of Mesnes confirmed that he had pledged never to be taken alive by the police.

GREAT BRITAIN

THE GREAT TRAIN ROBBERY

On 8 July 1965 train robber Ronnie Biggs was among four prisoners who escaped from London's Wandsworth Prison. Colleagues on the outside threw a ladder over the 30 ft prison wall and had three getaway cars waiting. As jail breaks go, the technique was simple but effective.

A Home Office spokesman later described what happened.

'At 3.05 pm one of the officers on duty in the yard saw a man's head appear above the outside wall. The officer immediately rang the alarm bell and at the same time the man on the wall threw over a rope and tubular ladder.

'The four prisoners immediately made for the ladder and climbed over the top. The prison officers tried to stop them, but were stopped by some of the others in the exercise yard. The officers went outside and discovered a van with a platform on top parked against

The Great Train Robbers, reunited some 30 years after their crime

the wall and the ladders secured to the top of the van.'

Police said that a green Ford Zephyr involved in the escape had been abandoned outside a nearby railway station. A loaded shotgun and a set of overalls were found inside.

Biggs had been one of the robbers that got away with £2.3 million in used one, five and ten-pound notes after holding up the Glasgow-to-Euston mail train at Bridego Bridge, Buckinghamshire. After rigging the signals, the 15-strong gang formed a human chain to off-load 120 bags of money and mail. Working by moonlight, they pulled off the biggest robbery ever investigated by Scotland Yard, which soon became known as 'The Great Train Robbery'.

Only one man was injured. The driver, Jack Mills, 58, was viciously coshed and forced, bleeding and frightened, to move the train up the tracks. So traumatized was he by the experience that he never worked again and died in 1970 having never fully recovered from the attack.

The gang fled to a farm in Oxfordshire where they played Monopoly with real money, blissfully unaware that they were leaving invaluable fingerprint evidence for the police.

Soon they were forced to scatter as the police closed in. Almost all were soon rounded up and received jail sentences that amounted to more than 300 years. One of those who eluded police at the time was Bruce Reynolds, the brains behind the raid. He was finally captured in 1969 and served ten years of a 25-

Great Train Robber Ronnie Biggs fled to Brazil where he lived in exile for many years

year sentence. Buster Edwards, the robber turned flower seller who was later the subject of a blockbuster movie, fled to Mexico where he remained for four years until giving himself up. He committed suicide in 1994.

Charlie Wilson escaped from Winson Green Prison in Birmingham the same year as Biggs, with help from someone who had copied the master key. He was recaptured four years later in Canada. After doing his time, he went to Spain, became involved in the drug scene and was shot by a hitman in 1990 as he reclined by his swimming pool.

Living the vida loca

As for Biggs, he underwent plastic surgery and went to Spain and Australia before settling in Brazil. After fathering a child with a Brazilian woman he was permitted to stay in the country. A kidnapping attempt and a new extradition treaty between Britain and Brazil failed to uproot him.

In one of the numerous interviews he gave during his fugitive years he acknowledged that he had been 'blessed with fantastic good luck over the years.'

He celebrated his 70th year with a party in Brazil attended by Bruce Reynolds, who was recovering from the effects of a stroke, and other noted criminals. Marking the occasion he was sent a handmade card by Charles Bronson – Britain's most notorious prisoner who had by that time spent 25 years in jail, mostly in solitary confinement – with the handwritten epithet: 'Never walk backwards into a madman's cage, especially if you are wearing a kilt'.

Bronson, jailed for seven years for armed robbery in 1974, has since been in 20 different prisons, eight rooftop protests, assaulted at least 20 prison officers, held 10 people as hostages – threatening to eat one – and caused at least £500,000 worth of damage to prison property. A shaven-headed artist and poet, his fitness regime included 2,500 press-ups a day. He was one of many members of the criminal fraternity at the party.

But eighteen months later Biggs decided to end his 40-year era of life on the run. He returned to Britain and a 30-year prison sentence, as yet unserved. He was sent to the high-security prison, HM Belmarsh, quietly hoping for a release before his 80th birthday.

Soviet spy George Blake. After escaping from Wormwood Scrubs prison in 1966, he eventually turned up in Moscow, where he remained for the rest of his life

Around the time of a renewed appeal a critically lauded album of his own jazz music, composed while in Brazil for a film he hoped would be made about his life, was released as *Mailbag Blues: Ronnie Biggs' Story*.

MOSCOW SPY

Wormwood Scrubs is one of London's Victorian prisons, familiar for the twin eight-sided towers that frame its entrance. The iconic gateway has featured in numerous movies and television series and has come to represent prisons to the British public.

More famous for its grim conditions than its inmates, it was nonetheless thrust into the spotlight in 1966 when its most controversial inmate, the spy George Blake, escaped to freedom.

Blake, 44, had served only five years of the 42-year sentence he received for spying for the Soviet Union. Once a trusted figure in government circles, Blake had been converted to Communism while a prisoner in North Korea during the Korean War. Sympathizers decided to bust him out of jail, believing the sentence harsh and hypocritical.

After removing a single bar from his cell window and using a ladder specially constructed with Size 13 knitting needles, Blake vanished into the night. He was kept in several safe houses before being transported to East Germany, at the time under a Communist regime, and then to Moscow where he was welcomed as a hero.

In 1990, two men, Michael Randle and Pat Pottle, were charged in connection with Blake's flight. Any doubts about what Randle and Pottle did 26 years previously were dispelled by the title of their recently published book *The Blake Escape: How We Freed George Blake and Why.* Yet the jury acquitted them of wrongdoing after they both delivered passionate speeches from the dock.

For his part, Blake stayed in the safety of Moscow from where he observed the collapse of Communism, a political system he so admired that he betrayed his own country.

USA

THE GOOD, THE BAD AND THE DANGEROUS

If there's a romance associated with prisoners then it is multiplied tenfold when it comes to escapees. But while some on the run appear to be good guys, some are downright evil.

The exploits of Frank Abagnale Jr. have passed into folklore, not least because they featured in the hit film, *Catch Me If You Can.* The movie, directed by Steven Spielberg and starring Leonardo DiCaprio and Tom Hanks, was inspired by the book of the same name, written by Abagnale and a ghost writer. The events were subject to exaggeration, claims Abagnale.

By his own admission, though, Abagnale got enmeshed in forgery and fraud at an early age after running away from home. By the time he was arrested in France at the age of 21 he had cashed $2.5 million worth of checks in 26 different countries and every American state.

His career in international travel began when he realized that it was customary for airlines to offer free seats to crew from rival companies so that they could fulfil flight obligations in foreign destinations. With the help of a counterfeit identity card and a stolen uniform he travelled the world without buying a ticket.

Master forger

If that wasn't enough, he became an attorney in Louisiana, a pediatrician in Georgia and a college professor at Brigham Young University after forging the necessary qualifications.

When he was arrested in France after being seen on a 'wanted' poster he was sent to prison in Perpignan where he suffered malnutrition and pneumonia. After six months he was passed on to Sweden where the prison conditions were altogether better. But facing deportation to the US on an array of charges he decided to escape from custody at the first opportunity. That happened to be when the landing gear on the plane he was traveling on went down as it approached JFK airport. Having garnered considerable experience of airline travel he had locked himself in the plane lavatory and dismantled the compartment, opening up a small hatch. As soon as the plane touched down he wriggled through the hole, jumped onto the tarmac and fled over the airport fence.

His destination was now Montreal where he had a considerable sum resting in a safe deposit box. Unfortunately for him, he was spotted by a Canadian border guard and re-arrested.

However, his ingenuity was by no means exhausted. As a prisoner at the Federal Detention Centre in Atlanta, Georgia, he

Leonardo DiCaprio stars as master fraudster Frank Abagnale Jr in the movie *Catch Me if You Can.*

managed to convince guards that he was in fact an undercover prison inspector. With help from an ex-girlfriend he produced paperwork to validate his claim and was finally released, supposedly to attend a meeting with an FBI agent. Intent on going to Brazil, he first returned to New York to tie up loose ends. Once again sharp-eyed law enforcement officers, this time in an unmarked police car, put an end to his plans.

He was distraught and depressed by the 12-year sentence he received in America. However, after five years he was offered a unique opportunity to help the government track down fraudsters. Although the job was unpaid, it meant freedom from incarceration at the age of 26. Abagnale eventually began a career advising banks and security firms about the techniques used by criminals. He remains wary of attempts to glamorize his past:

> 'Age brings wisdom and fatherhood changes one's life completely. I consider my past immoral, unethical and illegal. It is something I am not proud of. I am proud that I have been able to turn my life around.'

THE TEXAS SEVEN

Then there are escapees who are altogether less appealing. The gang that burst out of the John Connally Unit in Kenedy, Texas on 13 December 2000 falls very much into this category because they were armed and very dangerous.

The men involved were convicted armed robbers George Rivas and Donald Newbury, rapists Larry Harper and Patrick Murphy Jnr., murderers Michael Rodriguez and Joseph Garcia, and Randy Halprin, guilty of attacking a child.

Individually they were unremarkable convicts serving long sentences. Together they were silhouetted in the national spotlight when they became known as the Texas Seven.

Rivas was the brains behind the breakout and he worked out the details of a plan that called for the men to pose as civilian workers or impersonate guards. The real workers and guards were stripped, bound and gagged and left in a locked cupboard. It took more than two hours before everything was in place. Only then did two of the men, in disguise, enter a watch tower, overpower the guards, open the prison's back door, alerting the other escapees on the prison telephone system. The seven left in a truck belonging to the Texas Department of Correctional Justice (TDCJ), armed with weapons and ammunition stolen from the watch tower and leaving 13 hostages shocked but unharmed.

The escape plan was executed with some panache, although Glen Castlebury of the TDCJ was confident the convicts would be quickly re-captured. Out of the 275 inmates who had escaped from Texan prisons in the previous 16 years only one had not been caught.

'It may be a week, a month or three months but they're always back,' he declared.

His confidence was well-placed. Police cars littered the main highways and there were few places to hide in the flat farmland that surrounded Kenedy. The seven restocked with a robbery and lay low in a motel until they decided on another raid to assure their short-term future. The venue would be an Oshman's store in Irving, Texas; the date Christmas Eve.

Posing as security guards, three of the seven gathered the staff at the front counter when the shop was closing. Employees were bound and gagged although, crucially, left unharmed. Apart from cash the robbers took 60 semi-automatic handguns, shotguns and rifles.

They might have escaped into the night if it hadn't been for an off-duty employee whose suspicions were aroused by the events he watched unfold from the outside.

Christmas killing

Police officer Aubrey Hawkins was enjoying a meal with his wife and young son nearby. When the call came over the radio he jumped into his vehicle and headed for the rear door of Oshman's. Just as he pulled up the robbers emerged and started shooting. Before he even

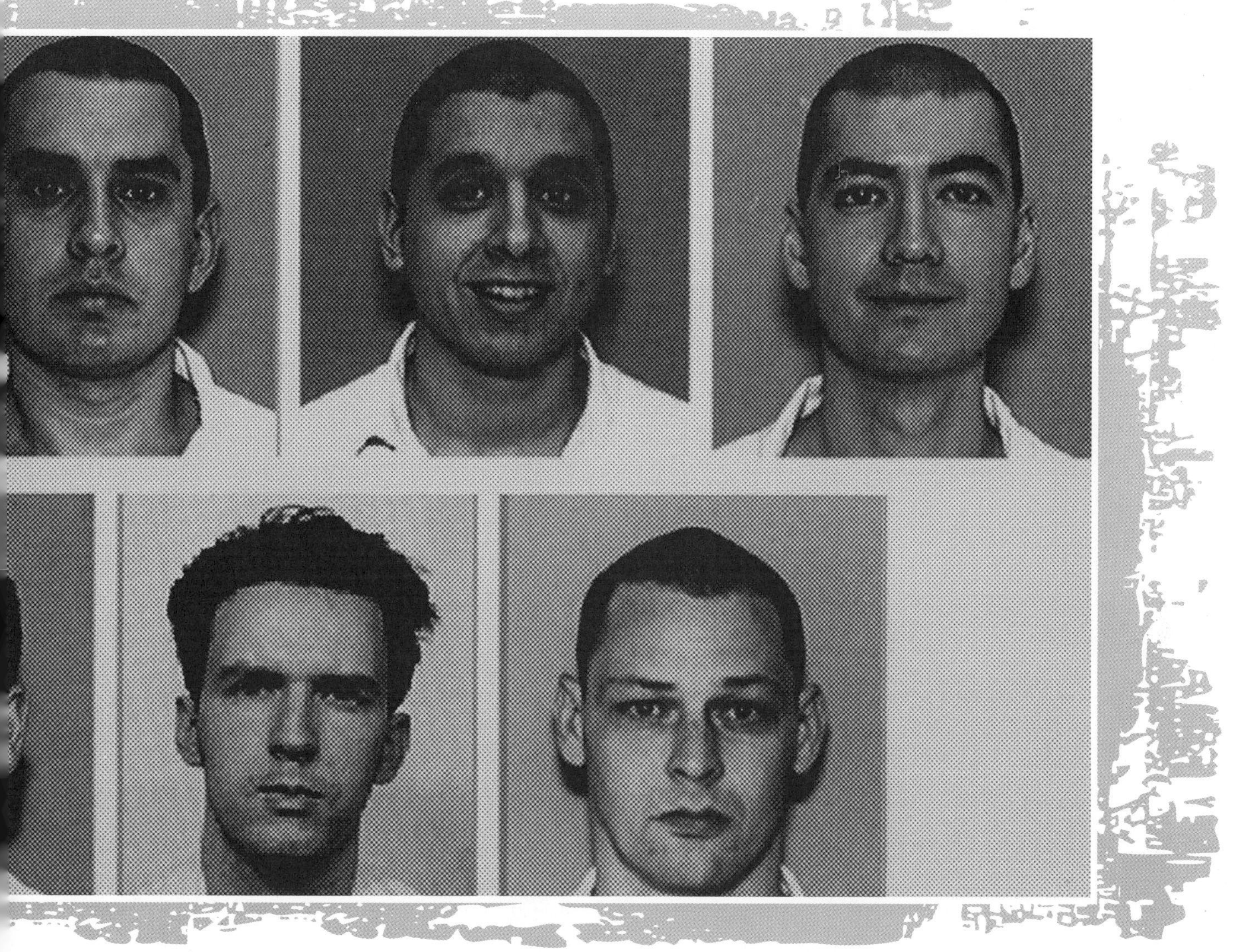

had a chance to open the car door, Hawkins was hit by a volley of bullets. As he reeled in agony, the men pulled him from his car and shot him again. As the fugitives screeched away, their vehicle ran over Officer Hawkins' head. He didn't survive the night.

The search for the seven now began in earnest. Despite national publicity and the offer of fat rewards for information there were no obvious leads for police to go on until the owner of a caravan park called. A Pace-Arrow RV parked at his premises in Colorado since the start of January contained seven men who claimed to be travelling Christians. They looked, however, very much like the Texas Seven. Police were swiftly in the vicinity, watching and waiting.

For safety's sake they couldn't stop two vehicles from leaving the site, but both were followed and intercepted and five of the convicts re-arrested. After that, the two men who remained in the RV were challenged by armed police. Randy Halprin, apparently injured in cross fire during the Christmas Eve robbery, limped out with his hands up. Harper, meanwhile, demanded to speak to his father, a highly-decorated Vietnam veteran but before the phone link up could be set up the honour student had shot himself in the head.

The six survivors were returned to Texas to face murder trials and – for Rivas, Newbury and Rodriguez at least – the bleakness of life on death row. Those three have all been sentenced to death but the date of their executions has not yet been fixed. The others will also have to wait – but for their trial dates. They can only guess at what their additional sentences will be.

In December 2000 seven men escaped from a prison in Texas, shooting a policeman 11 times while on the run. A reward of $100,000 each was offered for their capture

5

DEATH: THE ULTIMATE SANCTION

THE days of crucifixion on a bleak hilltop before jeering crowds are long gone. Deemed a humiliating way to die, this was reserved for those judged to be the most heinous villains, deserving of an agonizing and drawn out death.

Several thousand years after the era of crucifixion the death penalty remains with us, although today it's usually carried out behind closed doors and there's greater emphasis on minimizing the pain of the condemned.

The arguments for and against the death penalty are well worn. Those who support it believe men and women sentenced to death are getting a taste of their own medicine. Harsh treatment, they claim, will deter others from following the same evil path and offers closure to the grieving relatives of crime victims. Those against the death penalty claim that the process is an abomination of human rights. And what if someone is sent to their death when they are in fact innocent of the crime? The death penalty is handed down for murder, mirroring the Biblical 'eye for an eye' doctrine. Other crimes that are sometimes punishable by death include drug trafficking, adultery, armed robbery, kidnapping, rape, political crimes and, even, tax evasion and embezzlement. There is no international uniformity, however.

A priest looks on before a lethal injection is administered to convicted kidnapper and killer Tomas Cerrate in Guatemala

In China the legal code provides for the death penalty in no fewer than 28 different criminal arenas. It has popular public support in a country fond of the saying 'you should kill the chicken to scare the monkeys'.

Some Islamic countries, including Iran and Saudi Arabia, adhere to Sharia law, drawn from the Koran and incorporating the death penalty. It is a code of conduct rather than a judicial system of law and covers areas as diverse as marriage, trade and donations to the poor. Existing outside the checks and balances of any secular legal system, the treatment of evidence is sometimes thought to be dubious. However, Sharia law is subject to interpretation and so varies dramatically in implementation.

In America about three-quarters of the population apparently backs the death penalty although recent evidence suggests lessening support. Opponents cite numerous studies showing unequal application of capital punishment depending on factors like race and geographical region. The odds of a black man receiving the death penalty in Philadelphia, for example, are nearly four times the norm.

There are also doubts about the quality of legal assistance available to poor defendants. Laboratory analysis of blood or body fluids found at a crime scene cost money. So does legal representation. The best legal teams – the sort that might tear into a prosecutor's case and create doubt in the mind of a jury – are extraordinarily expensive and few who find themselves in court on a murder rap can afford a proven team.

As Clive Stafford Smith, the renowned British-born lawyer who fights for those on Death Row, points out: 'It's true to say that if you get competent representation at trial then, short of a lightning bolt from the sky, you don't get the death penalty.'

And many more people are found guilty of murder than face the death penalty, even in states that have capital punishment on the statute books.

Only 38 of America's 50 states retain the death penalty and it is used more often in some states than in others. Texas tends to have the highest execution rate while California generally has the most populated Death Row.

Perhaps because of the issues surrounding the death penalty or a subtle switch in popular culture, the execution rate in the US has been falling. In 2006 there were 12 per cent fewer executions than in 2005 – and 46 per cent fewer than in 1999. Only 14 of the 38 states carried out an execution and just six more than one. A sentence of life without parole often finds favour with juries who are reluctant to determine whether someone lives or dies. The rate of violent crime is also falling in the US, although it's difficult to say whether or not this has a bearing on the figures.

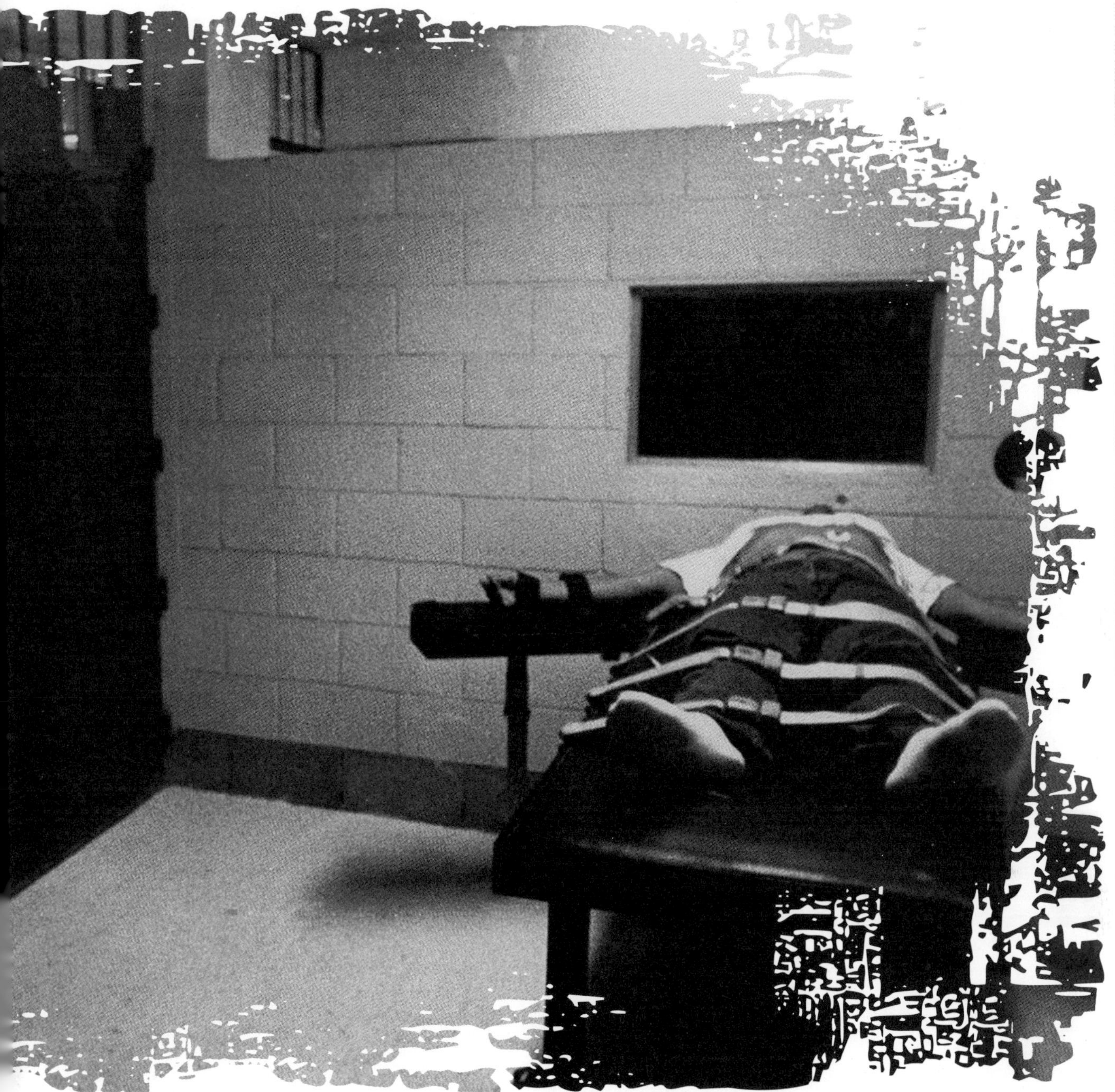

Of course, just because the death penalty exists on the statute books doesn't mean it must be used. But if it is there it can be wielded for its deterrent factor as part of the fight against crime. This is evident in China where there have been several 'strike hard' campaigns, in a bid to reduce the crime figures, which have resulted in a bulge in the execution figures.

At the present time, those condemned to death have died at the behest of the state by hanging, shooting, electrocution, lethal injection and stoning.

LETHAL INJECTION

At 6.13pm on 25 October 2006 Danny Rolling – the Gainesville Ripper – breathed his last breath after being pumped full of deadly drugs in Starke Prison's death chamber, in Florida.

He had admitted killing five students in just a few days in Florida in 1990 using a hunting knife. The court heard how he caught a Greyhound bus to Gainesville, pitched a tent near some woods and set out on a murderous spree with the sole intention of becoming a 'superstar' among serial killers.

Convicted murderer J.D. Autry waits on death row in Huntsville State Prison, Texas, some months before he was executed by lethal injection

After killing and, in some cases, sexually assaulting his victims he posed their bodies in macabre positions as if to underline his sensational brutality.

Artifacts and DNA linked Rolling to the grisly crimes. He insisted childhood abuse by his policeman father caused him to suffer multiple personalities. However, investigators were suspicious when he labeled his murderous personality 'Gemini', the same name given to the killer in the film *Exorcist III*, a movie Rolling watched shortly before his deadly spree. After being sentenced to death Rolling confessed to a further three killings.

When the sentence was imminent, Rolling told a news agency: 'I do deserve to die, but do I want to die? No, I want to live. Life is difficult to give up.'

In the two minutes offered to him to make a statement, he sang a hymn that he had apparently penned himself and continued to sing until the drugs took effect.

After he had expired, Dianne Hoyt, whose stepdaughter was among his victims, put

forward a different point of view: 'This man brought this outcome on himself and the law of the land carried through to show us justice.'

Lethal cocktail

Since 1982 lethal injection has been the preferred option by US states for the purposes of capital punishment. Enthusiasm for it has spread to other nations, who have willingly swapped other methods of death for this ostensibly quick and clean alternative.

The condemned are fed a cocktail of drugs – sodium thiopental to induce sleep; pancuronium bromide, a muscle relaxant that collapses the lungs; and potassium chloride to stop the heart – delivered in short order via an intravenous tube. A heart monitor attached to the prisoner gives prison staff and medical observers a further insight into the progress of the execution.

A specially-trained medical team, not the prison warden, is responsible for putting the syringes in place to make sure the process is swift and painless for both prisoner and staff. It is this aspect of death by lethal injection that troubles some campaigners in favour of the death penalty. They argue that the convict does not suffer in the way their victims did and so the deterrent factor is lost.

Prison chaplain Jim Brazzil recalled the death of one man that illustrates the astonishing speed of the drugs:

> 'He made his final statement and then after the warden gave the signal he started singing Silent Night, and he got to the point "Round yon virgin mother and child" and just as he got "child" out, that was the last word.'

for much of the time and struggled, groaning in agony.

Four years later, in the same state, Raymond Landry's execution was disrupted when the catheter popped out of his vein, spraying lethal substances around the room. It took 24 minutes for him to die. Afterwards, a spokesman for the Texas Department of Corrections said: 'There was something of a delay in the execution because of what officials call a "blow out". The syringe came out from the vein and the warden ordered the team to re-inject the catheter into the vein.'

In 1989, again in Texas, Stephen McCoy reacted violently when the drugs were administered. One witness fainted as McCoy writhed in agony, apparently suffocating in response to the second drug as it paralysed his

I do deserve to die, but do I want to die? No, I want to live. Life is difficult to give up.

As commentator Deborah Denno has indicated: 'Some proponents [of capital punishment] feel that [lethal] injection can save the death penalty from abolition while some opponents believe injection can save inmates from torture.'

A painful end

The sanitized nature of lethal injection has prompted some prisoners to choose alternatives to highlight what they perceive to be the barbarity of capital punishment. But their faith in the efficacy of lethal injection might be misplaced.

In fact, executions do not always go to plan and there have been plenty of examples of prisoners ending their lives in agony.

When James Autry was put to death in Texas, in 1984, the first two drugs reacted to one another and solidified in the catheter. Autry remained conscious as the medical team worked to re-instate the drug supply. A witness for *Newsweek* magazine reported that Autry took at least ten minutes to die, was conscious

lungs. Afterwards, prison authorities conceded the injection could have been administered in either a heavier dose or more rapidly.

In Missouri in 1995 the straps holding Emmitt Foster down were so tight that the drugs could not circulate around his body. It took 30 minutes for him to die.

Those examples aside, a fairly common difficulty presented to the medical team concerns prisoners who have been long-term drug users. Their veins have often collapsed and are difficult to penetrate. Frequently, a prisoner's last act is offering to locate a vein to speed up the process.

All these cases, and others, have raised the possibility that lethal injection is against America's Eighth Amendment, which prohibits cruel and unusual punishment. And, while the muscle relaxants make prisoners appear serene, are they in fact in great pain but unable to express it? The argument has found some favour in America's courtrooms, notably in California where the use of an initial sleeping draught for prisoners is being investigated.

An 1890 engraving from the *Scientific American* shows the first execution by electric chair, which took place on 6 August that year

China is beginning to turn its attention to lethal injection, seeing it as a more modern option to its present method – a bullet in the back of the head. Although it was brought to China in 1997, the number of facilities equipped for lethal injection remains limited. However, the recent introduction of fully-equipped mobile vans has increased the rate of executions by lethal injection. There are fewer costs as, unlike public executions, these don't need input from numerous armed guards.

An added incentive for change comes from the fact that the Chinese harvest organs from the bodies of the executed, which are used in high-value trade, usually without seeking permission from the prisoners or their relatives. The preference is clearly for lethal injection as the body parts remain in better condition than if the donor is shot.

ELECTRIC CHAIR

In 1998 Gerald Eugene Stano was sent to Florida's electric chair for stabbing to death a 17-year-old female hitch hiker. She was one of more than 40 women killed by Stano in at least three states. Stano, adopted at 13 months, failed at school and was fired from menial jobs for petty theft or obnoxious behaviour.

In his 20s he began a career in killing that outlasted all his other interests. Canny police work following a vicious attack on a prostitute finally put him behind bars aged 29.

Stano made no final statement and stared fixedly ahead during his execution, managing just a glimmer of a smile at his attorney.

Three feet away, behind the witness viewing window, Raymond Neal anxiously watched the man who killed his sister, Ramona.

Later he told reporters from the Associated Press: 'The power slammed into him and he jerked as much as he could and that was it. I saw the life going out of his hands. It felt like a ton of bricks had been lifted off my back. Afterward, me and my brothers smoked cigars to celebrate.

'I can't express the feeling. I felt so much better. I'm so glad Florida has the guts to keep the electric chair.'

Industrial rivalry

Nineteenth-century America was the birthplace of electricity and, by chance, this innovation coincided with a move to find new, more humane methods of execution. Soon electricity and the death penalty were joined together, bringing forth a new method of capital punishment dubbed 'electrocution'.

Much of the groundwork was laid by Thomas Edison (1847-1931), who flirted with the invention of light bulbs in 1879 and, by 1884, had devised an electricity generating and supply system. However, he was not alone in pioneering electrical innovation and it was his rivalry with George Westinghouse (1846-1914) that finally led to the creation of the electric chair.

In essence, Edison had created a system for Direct Current (DC) electricity while Westinghouse backed his own projects that used Alternate Current (AC). After 1886, when a commission in New York was formed to investigate new ways of carrying out the death penalty, the highly-competitive Edison was determined to prove that AC was the more dangerous of the two methods, hoping to ensure that his invention became the preferred choice for homes.

Despite personal objections to capital punishment, he secretly employed scientist Harold Brown to carry out macabre public experiments, using a second-hand Westinghouse generator, to highlight the perils of AC.

Later Westinghouse recalled: 'I remember Tom [Edison] telling them that direct current was like a river flowing peacefully to the sea, while alternating current was like a torrent rushing violently over a precipice. Imagine that! Why they even had a professor named Harold Brown who went around talking to audiences... and electrocuting dogs and old horses right on stage, to show how dangerous alternating current was.'

Usually, stray cats and dogs were killed, but the most high-profile victim of this commercial jostling was Topsy the Elephant, presumably redundant from her previous role at a circus. It was at this stage that Edison coined the term 'electrocution'.

Edison's covert crusade was sufficient to persuade the New York commission to introduce legislation in 1889, known as the Electric Execution Law, to make electrocution the state's official solution to the death penalty conundrum, as it was deemed quicker and kinder than hanging.

Brown went on to develop the electric chair and it was ready for use by 1890. Acutely aware of the damage electrocution might do to his business interests, Westinghouse funded the appeals made by the first scheduled victim, wife-killer William Kemmler, on the grounds that it was 'cruel and unusual' punishment, thus contrary to the American Constitution's Eighth Amendment.

But his efforts failed and Kemmler was executed on 6 August of that year at Auburn Prison, New York. Despite its promise of a swift, painless death, witnesses were horrified by what they saw. The technicians misjudged the current needed to kill a man and the first jolt left Kemmler singed but alive. Only after a second shock did he die. One reporter who witnessed the execution described it as 'an awful spectacle, much worse than hanging' while Westinghouse commented that they would have done better to use an axe. Efforts by Edison to describe the process as being 'Westinghoused' came to nothing.

Harm chair

Although advances in electrical engineering were exported from America across the world, the electric chair remained very much an American phenomenon, with the sole exception of the Philippines.

By 1906 more than 100 people had been dispatched by electric chairs at three New York prisons: Auburn, Clinton and Sing Sing. After 1914 all electric chair executions took place at Sing Sing. The device was adopted in 26 other

The electric chair at New York's Sing Sing prison, photographed in 1940

Lawyers acting for condemned prisoners Ruth Snyder and Henry Judd Gray, surrounded by journalists, wait outside New York's Sing Sing prison for confirmation of their clients' execution

states where it became known as Sizzlin' Sally, Old Smokey, Old Sparky, Yellow Mama, the Hot Squat or Gruesome Gertie.

Before the procedure begins the prisoner's head and legs are shaved so that the electrodes, moistened with saline solution or gel to prevent burning, can be better fixed in place. He or she is then strapped to a strongly-constructed chair by arm, leg and chest straps. The prisoner is not sedated. The process of fixing the straps is carried out by a team and takes only 45 seconds.

A first shock of about 2,000 volts is intended to kill. It is nevertheless followed by up to three more blasts of electricity to ensure the job is done. After the second shock there's

usually a five-minute gap so that a doctor can check for signs of life.

Obviously, the effect on a human body is catastrophic. The voltage is intended to cause paralysis so that heart function is rendered impossible. However, it also cooks the internal organs. In 1985 Justice William Brennan revealed: 'When the post-electrocution autopsy is perform the liver is so hot that doctors say it cannot be touched by the human hand.'

A mask is always used to cover the face of those in the chair because of the horrifying effects the electrical charges have on the eyeballs. Most victims also wear incontinence protection.

Julius and Ethel Rosenberg after the trial that found them guilty of spying for the Soviet Union. Both were later executed

Public fascination with this method of death has always been rampant. It was fuelled in 1928 when an execution witness wearing a camera around his ankle snapped murderess Ruth Snyder at Sing Sing just as the electric charge activated. Snyder and her lover, Judd

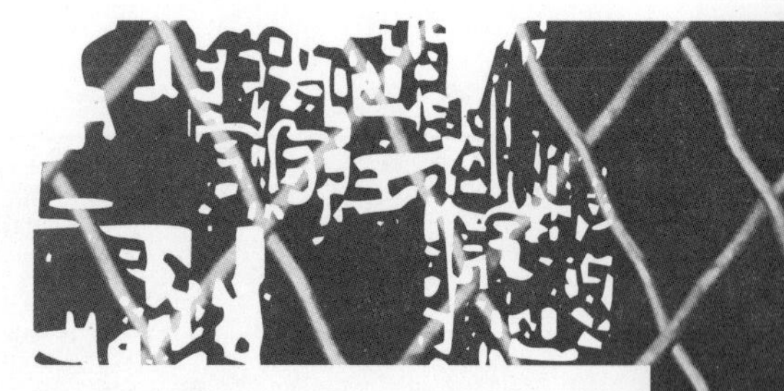

I have thrown the switch which has hurled into eternity 387 occupants of the electric chair

Gray, had murdered her husband and tried to make it seem like a random killing. Both were swiftly arrested, however, and the case attracted immense publicity.

When the picture appeared on the front of the *New York Daily News* it was the hot topic of the day. That Judd Gray's feet flared up in flames during his execution barely warranted a mention.

The man responsible for their deaths was the official Sing Sing executioner, Robert G Elliott, who noted in his autobiography, *Agent of Death*: 'I have thrown the switch which has hurled into eternity 387 occupants of the electric chair.'

Paradoxically, Elliott professed to being opposed to capital punishment but saw himself carrying out a necessary job at the behest of the state. Indeed, it was not the task that disturbed him so much as the baying crowds that gathered outside a prison at execution times. 'Many in those throngs were morbid individuals, to whom death is a commonplace jest and human life is cheap.'

Details have been released to a sensation-seeking public from witnesses to the event.

A reporter, Mike James, described rapist Ray Anderson's death in the electric chair in 1939:

'Out of consideration for the executioner the room in which he pulls the switch is usually separated from the chair by a wall or partition. This is supposed to make the puller of the death lever

feel more clinical and impersonal about it — less guilty.

'The warden raised his hand. The executioner in the next room closed the circuit. There was a hum, like a diesel train getting underway; an unreal bluish light filled the room. The man in the chair rose as if to get up quickly and run out but he was stopped abruptly, jolting in mid-air by the restraining straps. His body, straining against the straps, seemed about to burst them and take flight. His hair sparked and sizzled with bluish flame for an instant. Then the humming sound stopped; 2,200 volts dropped out from under him and he slumped back into the chair, no longer a man but a body.'

Shocking stories

High-profile criminals who have met their end in the electric chair include spies Julius and Ethel Rosenberg, who were blamed by their trial judge for thousands of American deaths in the Korean War. Ethel Rosenberg, apparently guilty of nothing more than typing up notes and stoic loyalty to her husband and friends, died with Julius on 19 June 1953 after three electrical jolts. After the first failed to kill her, there was a wait as the straps were re-applied. Sons Michael and Robert learned of their deaths through a radio broadcast.

Leon Czologz, the assassin of President William McKinley in 1901, used his last words to affirm his guilt. 'I killed the President because he was the enemy of the good people – the good working people. I am not sorry for my crime.' But as the prison guards strapped him into the chair, he did say through clenched teeth, 'I am sorry I could not see my father.'

Bruno Hauptmann, convicted of killing aviator Charles Lindbergh's baby after a bungled kidnap attempt, went to the electric chair in 1936 protesting his innocence. The only positive he could identify was that the end of capital punishment was in sight. 'Should, however, my death serve for the purpose of abolishing capital punishment – such a punishment being arrived at only by circumstantial evidence – I feel that my death has not been in vain.'

Serial sex killer Ted Bundy also went to the electric chair. The suave graduate confessed to 30 murders and was suspected of many more. After two escapes he was finally brought to trial in 1978 and, after conducting his own defense, was found guilty and sentenced to death.

The day before he died at Starke Prison, Gainesville, Florida, Bundy was interviewed by psychologist Dr James Dobson. His death, Bundy said, would satisfy society's desire for retribution but would do nothing to curtail the threat from those like him who were fuelled by a fatal combination of alcohol and hard-core pornography.

'I can't say that being in the Valley of the Shadow of Death is something I've become all that accustomed to, and that I'm strong and nothing's bothering me. It's no fun. It gets kind of lonely, yet I have to remind myself that every one of us will go through this someday in one way or another.'

The interview was interrupted when the lights dimmed momentarily as prison officials tested the chair before Bundy was strapped into it.

Yet the electric chair is most often recalled for the executions that went wrong. The state of Georgia found itself in the spotlight after the botched execution of Alpha Otis Stephens in 1984.

Dick Pettys of the Associated Press described the Stephens execution: 'Seconds after a mask was placed over [Stephens's] head, the first jolt was applied, causing his body to snap forward and his fists to clench. His body slumped when the current stopped two minutes later, but shortly afterward, witnesses saw him struggle to breathe. During the required six minutes in which the body was allowed to cool before doctors could examine it, Stephens took about 23 breaths. At 12:26 am, two doctors examined Stephens and said he was alive. At the second jolt, administered at 12:28 am, Stephens again snapped upright. The charge was discontinued at 12:30 am, and at 12:36 am, he was pronounced dead.'

An eyewitness account of Alabama's electrocution of John Louis Evans on 12 April 1983 outlined the protracted event.

'At 8:30 pm the first jolt of 1,900 volts of electricity passed through Mr Evans' body. It lasted thirty seconds. Sparks and flames erupted from the electrode tied to Mr Evans' left leg. His body slammed against the straps holding him in the electric chair and his fist clenched permanently. The electrode apparently burst from the strap holding it in place. A large puff of greyish smoke and sparks poured out from under the hood that covered Mr Evans' face. An overpowering stench of burnt flesh and clothing began pervading the witness room. Two doctors examined Mr Evans and declared that he was not dead.

'The electrode on the left leg was refastened. Mr. Evans was administered a second thirty-second jolt of electricity. The stench of burning flesh was nauseating. More smoke emanated from his leg and head. Again, the doctors examined Mr. Evans. The doctors reported that his heart was still beating, and that he was still alive.'

An overpowering stench of burnt flesh and clothing began pervading the witness room. Two doctors examined Mr Evans and declared that he was not dead

In Arkansas 61-year-old F.G. Bullen survived electrocution. As one witness reported: 'We placed the body in the coffin and the undertaker was preparing to replace the lid, when suddenly I heard him gasp and saw him turn pale. "My God!" he whispered. "Look!"

'I looked at the figure in the coffin. Bullen breathed and stirred in the casket. We called the warden, and guards carried the limp figure back to the electric chair, strapped it in, and the electrician administered the current for five more minutes.'

The smell of burning flesh

Smoke emanating from the contact points is not unusual, nor is the odour of burning flesh. However, when Pedro Medina was executed in Florida in 1997 flames leapt from the helmet containing the electrical contacts on his head. Three years after that, convicted police killer Jesse Tafero was also engulfed in flames and smoke after voltage was reduced following difficulties with the electrical connections.

One of the most terrifying cases occurred in 1946 when Willie Francis, aged 17, survived the chair. A witness reported:

'I heard the one in charge yell to the man outside for more juice when he saw that Willie Francis was not dying, and the one on the outside yelled back he was giving him all he had.'

The episode came to an end when Francis cried out, 'Take it off, let me breathe'.

Photographed in 1946, Willie Francis calmly reads a book after the electric chair failed to kill him. He was successfully executed a year later

Later Francis said: 'I felt a burning in my head and my left leg and I jumped against the straps. I saw little blue and pink and green speckles.'

Despite this appalling ordeal, Francis was given another date with the electric chair a year later, which on that occasion worked as intended.

Two of the key problems identified with existing electric chairs are their age – costs to refurbish are astronomical – and human error in application.

Nevertheless, they are still in use. In Nebraska it is the only option for capital punishment. And on 20 July 2006 Brandon Wayne Hendrick died in the electric chair in Virginia having chosen it in preference to a lethal injection. Hendrick, the killer of a 23-year-old woman, was the first person to die in the electric chair in the US since 2004.

GAS CHAMBER

On 30 January 1998 Ricky Lee Sanderson was executed by lethal gas at Central Prison in Raleigh, North Carolina, for stabbing a 16-year-old girl to death in 1985. Dressed in only white boxer shorts and wearing a leather mask to hide facial contortions, Sanderson died at 2.19 am, 18 minutes after the gas was released.

Sanderson kidnapped teenager Sue Ellen Holliman when he found her alone and sick in a house he planned to burgle. Later he raped her, forced her into the trunk of his car and drove to an isolated spot where he dug a shallow grave before choking and stabbing her. He resorted to murder to prevent her from revealing his car license plate number.

Curiously, another man had already confessed to the killing before Sanderson, in prison on unrelated charges, told police what had happened. He did so after discovering a strong religious faith behind bars.

Having been on death row for nearly 13 years, the 38-year-old Sanderson waived his right to further appeals. Although he had the option of lethal injection he chose the gas chamber – used in North Carolina since 1936 – so that Sue Ellen's parents could witness his suffering. His last words were, 'I'm dying for a deed I did and I deserve death for it and I'm glad. Christ forgive me.'

Pig style

As with the electric chair, the quest for a humane alternative to hanging was the rationale behind the development of the gas chamber. It was first used in 1924, in Nevada, to execute killer Gee Jon. Having settled on the notion of gassing the guilty, prison wardens tried to administer the punishment while Jon slept in his cell. In hindsight, it was no great surprise that this approach failed and that a purpose-built gas chamber was required.

Initial experiments of the early gas chambers used pigs as victims and there were almost immediate calls for its abandonment after one reporter branded it more barbarous than being hung, drawn and quartered. While those being executed tended to be swiftly rendered unconscious, death did not occur until 15 minutes or more after the gas was activated, making it the most protracted of all the capital punishment methods.

America's gas chambers look similar as most were made by the same company, Eaton Metal Products of Denver, Colorado. Made of welded and riveted steel, they are hexagonal in shape, standing eight feet high and six feet wide with five windows – for the benefit of execution witnesses and warden controllers.

Inside there is a chair (sometimes two), beneath which lies a pan containing sulphuric acid mixed with distilled water. Suspended above the liquid is a bag of cyanide crystals. Using a lever, the executioner releases the crystals into the acid and a cloud of deadly gas begins to rise and engulf the prisoner.

Death occurs when the gas stops oxygen from reaching the brain. Before this happens, the body generally jerks with uncontrollable spasms. It is thought that the pain suffered by the victim is similar to that experienced during heart attacks. The efficacy of the gas chamber depends in part on the victim: death will be swifter if he or she inhales deeply. However, most hold their breath for as long as possible.

Before being sealed inside the gas chamber the prisoner is fitted with two heart monitors by a doctor who uses them to assess the point of death.

Afterwards there's a time lapse while the poisonous fumes are extracted from the death chamber via a tall chimney. Even so, the first guards in must wear fully-protective clothing to avoid contamination. It's their job to ruffle the hair of the dead man to release any trapped gases, wash the corpse down with ammonia and destroy gas-ridden clothing.

Not every state adopted the gas chamber as its mode of death and only five still retain it as an option. California ruled it illegal in 1994.

It certainly may not be as humane as its pioneers had hoped. On 2 September 1983, during the execution of Jimmy Lee Gray in Mississippi, officials had to clear the witness room eight minutes after the gas was released when Gray's desperate gasps for air repulsed witnesses. According to the Death Penalty Information Center, his attorney, Dennis Balske, of Montgomery, Alabama, criticized state officials for emptying the room when the inmate was still alive.

On Penalty of Death...

'I'm going home, babe.'

— James Allen Red Dog, executed by lethal injection in Delaware, 1993

'I suppose resuscitation is out of the question.'

— Garry Miller after the warden asked if there was anything else that could be done for him prior to his execution in Texas in December 2000

'Remember, the death penalty is murder.'

— Robert Drew, executed by lethal injection in Texas, 1994

'I love you.' (Spoken to the executioner)

— Sean Flannagan, executed by lethal injection in New York, 1989

'How about this for a headline for tomorrow's paper – "French fries"?'

— James French, executed in the electric chair in Oklahoma, 1966

'I'd rather be fishing.'

— Jimmy Glass, executed in the electric chair in Louisiana, 1987

'I'd like to thank my family for loving me and taking care of me. And the rest of the world can kiss my ass.'

— Johnny Frank Garrett, Sr., executed by lethal injection in Texas, 1992

'I did not get my Spaghetti-O's, I got spaghetti. I want the press to know this.'

— Thomas J Grasso, executed by lethal injection in Oklahoma, 1995

'You can be a king or a street sweeper, but everyone dances with the Grim Reaper.'

— Robert Alton Harris, the last person executed in the gas chamber in California, 1992

'I don't hold any grudges. This is my doing. Sorry it happened.'

— Steven Judy, executed in the electric chair in Indiana, 1981

'Capital punishment: them without the capital get the punishment.'

— John Spenkelink, executed in the electric chair in Florida, 1979

'Well folks, you'll soon see a baked Appel.'

— Gangster George Appel, executed in the electric chair in New York, 1928

The airtight door to the gas chamber at San Quentin prison opens to show the chair within

Demonstrators against capital punishment (including actor Marlon Brando) outside the gates of San Quentin, on 2 May 1960, the day of convict-author Caryl Chessman's execution

Defense attorney David Bruck remarked: 'Jimmy Lee Gray died banging his head against a steel pole in the gas chamber while the reporters counted his moans (eleven, according to the Associated Press).'

In 1992, when Arizona used its gas chamber for the first time in a decade, witnesses branded it 'gruesome'. A UN Human Rights Committee, silent on electrocution, has branded the gas chamber 'a technique . . . considered to be torture or inhumane treatment.'

The high cost of gas

One of the biggest issues for the states that still keep a gas chamber is the cost of maintenance. Most are now more than sixty years old. Any degeneration in the effectiveness of the seals, for example, poses a threat to both prisoner and those in the vicinity during his execution.

The last execution by lethal gas carried out in the US took place in Arizona in 1999 when German national, Walter LaGrand, was dispatched despite legal maneuvers at the United Nations to halt the process.

Among those killed in the gas chamber was Caryl Chessman, known as the 'Red Light Bandit'. Convicted of rape rather than murder, Chessman became a reformed character after his arrest in 1948. He emerged a student of law (primarily to secure his future), a bar-room philosopher and an author. He wrote about his 'dogged and seemingly endless battle for survival' and once remarked: 'I don't mind dying, I just don't like being told when.'

His impressive efforts came to an end in the confines of the gas chamber on 2 May 1960. A last-minute call that would have postponed the hour of death came through just as the deadly gas had been released, and the warden decided it was too late to abandon the process. The signal Chessman had agreed with watching reporters to indicate whether the procedure was painful was given several times.

Convicted murderer Caryl Chessman holds a press conference in San Quentin prison, California, while awaiting execution in the gas chamber

Another high-profile victim was Barbara Graham, found guilty of killing a widow in her pursuit of loot. She was a mother of three who may have been framed for the murder, but she lost public sympathy by attempting to bribe her way to an alibi. Her route to the chamber was particularly agonizing.

Ready to make her last journey at 10 am, her appointment was delayed by two last-minute stays of execution that eventually came to nothing. 'Why do they torture me so? I was ready to die at 10 o'clock,' she wept. As she was strapped to the chair a guard tried to comfort her by saying she would feel no pain if she breathed deeply. 'How the hell would you know?' she retorted.

She asked for a blindfold in a bid to retain some dignity before execution witnesses. Her

last words were reportedly: 'Good people are always so sure they are right.'

Overseas, gas chambers were infamously used by Nazi Germany during the Second World War to kill millions of people that Hitler's regime had deemed to be undesirables. Today it is understood that they may be in use in North Korea, another totalitarian regime with a brutal record.

FIRING SQUAD

The dreary grey dawn that crept over the soft-stone buildings of Poperinghe, Belgium on 10 December 1916 was shattered when a volley of gunshots rang out from inside the town hall courtyard. The body of 31-year-old Eric Poole folded against a wooden post, the white target marking his heart soaked in blood, and the first British officer shot for desertion during the First World War was dead.

Second Lieutenant Eric Skeffington Poole, born in Nova Scotia and serving with the West Yorkshires, had an unblemished war record until he sustained head injuries following a shell explosion in the summer of 1916. Afterwards his behaviour became increasingly erratic although he was passed as fit for active service.

During a push on the front line at the Somme Poole was discovered wandering aimlessly behind the lines, some considerable distance from the men he was supposed to be leading. He told a court martial: 'I, at times, get confused and have great difficulty making up my mind.'

Nonetheless he was sentenced to death as punishment for his cowardice. A medical tribunal assembled to examine his case confirmed the order although it noted that his mental powers were 'less than average'. Sir Douglas Haig (1861-1928), Commander-in-Chief of the British Expeditionary Force and final arbiter of the case, denied Poole clemency, believing 'such a crime is more serious in the case of an officer than a man and it is also highly important that all ranks should realize the law is the same for an officer as a private'.

Despite Poole's obvious illness, his case and many others won little sympathy at home. Indeed, the burden of having a relative shot at dawn for cowardice weighed heavily.

No photos exist of a British serviceman being shot by his former comrades, although executions of German spies were captured on film. Conditions that the men experienced at the front are infamous, however. Troops had little sleep, ate spartan meals, wore lice-infested clothes and existed in perpetual fear of death. There were numerous examples of what is now called Post Traumatic Stress

A prisoner's eye view of a firing squad in the 1920s

Syndrome, which at the time was probably the condition known as 'shell-shock'.

In August 2006 all 306 men shot at dawn by the British during the Great War were posthumously pardoned by the British government, bringing to an end some nine decades of stigma.

The plight of men like Poole, reduced to physical and mental wrecks by the intensity of the Western Front bombardments, was highlighted in the long-running campaign that preceded the pardon. The fact that British desertions were running at the rate of about 1,000 a month at the height of hostilities and

that Haig pardoned nine out of ten men sentenced to death has been little publicized. There are those who still maintain the pardon was both sentimental and wrong, carried out by those re-inventing the past.

At the time, firing squads were considered the norm. The firing squad has been used as a judicial device since firearms developed an acceptable level of accuracy. Historically, it has been linked to military executions although it is the method of choice to dispatch convicted felons in several countries today including Yemen, Vietnam, North Korea and the Palestinian Authority. In China, felons are still frequently put to death by a bullet to the back of the head delivered by a policeman, often at a public rally held in a sports stadium or large public venue. By tradition, the officer will then demand the price of the bullet from the dead man's relatives.

Death by firing squad remains legal in two American states.

Gun crime

Firing squads may be swift and inexpensive, but as a method of execution there is something about them that is decidedly old hat.

In Dublin, Irish nationalists sought to take advantage of Britain's preoccupation with the Western Front during the First World War by sparking an uprising in 1916 that would secure independence from the British Empire. Initial hopes that the British would capitulate were quickly dashed when reinforcements came pouring over the Irish Sea. Ultimately, the ill-armed and sparse forces that sought to win an independent Ireland surrendered only days after the rebellion began.

The destination for the presumed ringleaders of the revolt was Kilmainham Gaol, built in 1796 to replace the former city prison which had been little more than a stinking pit. In the eyes of the British, who then ruled Ireland, the men were, quite simply, traitors and the penalty was death. So in May 1916 the men were executed by firing squad within the walls of the jail. One man, James Connolly, an eminent Socialist and philosopher, had been so badly injured during the fighting that he was tied to a chair before being shot in order that he remain upright.

In fact, the Easter Uprising, as it became known, had little popular support but the brutality of the British response elevated its main players to heroes and helped pave the way to Irish independence.

One of the leaders of the uprising, Eamon de Valera, was the last prisoner to be held at Kilmainham, which closed in 1924. He went on to become a long-serving Taoiseach (prime minister) and president of the Irish Republic.

The firing squad was also used by the French during the First World War as the penalty for those convicted of espionage. This included Mata Hari, the Dutch-born dancer

found guilty in 1916 of spying for the Germans. Taken before a firing squad at dawn, she waved away a priest and refused a blindfold before being shot.

In the Second World War German spy Josef Jakobs was the last person to be executed in the Tower of London, the scene of many state-sanctioned killings through the centuries. He was shot on 15 August 1941 after being found guilty of treachery for having parachuted into Britain with a radio in an attaché case, a revolver and nearly five

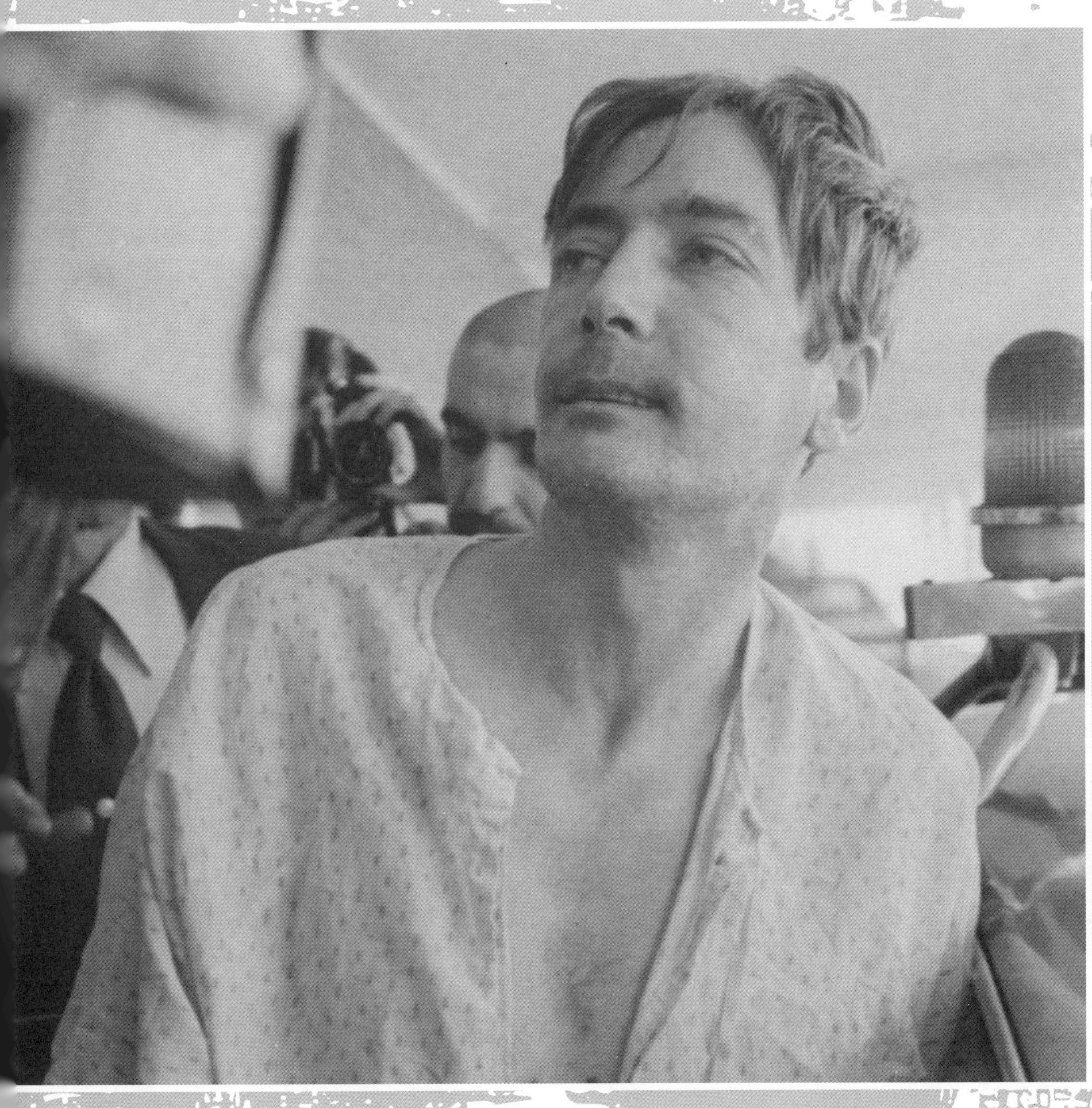

Courting celebrity, Gary Gilmore insisted he be executed, even firing his legal team when they tried to lodge an appeal at his sentence

hundred pounds. He used the gun to summon help after injuring his leg in the jump. His precise purpose remains unclear.

Looking through Gary Gilmore's eyes

The ten-year moratorium on the death penalty in the US ended in dramatic style with the shooting of Gary Gilmore. Although the story was in itself immense, headlines were ignited by Gilmore's determination to die.

Gilmore had been convicted, following a two-day trial, of murdering a motel manager. He was suspected of another killing as well. During his comparatively brief spell on Death Row, Gilmore twice attempted suicide. There was speculation at the time and since that he sought publicity rather than a swift death at his own hand as he clearly relished the celebrity that accompanied his position. Ultimately, there was no doubting his resolve. He fired his

The executioner's view of the seat used by firing squad victim Gary Gilmore at Point of the Mountain, Utah in 1977. The firing squad was hidden from Gilmore by a canvas screen

legal team when they prepared an appeal against his wishes. Indeed, when it seemed the law was ready to block his execution yet again he offered to pay for it himself.

To those who vigorously pursued legal measures to prevent his death, including the American Civil Liberties Union (ACLU), he said: 'Butt out, this is my life and it is my death.'

This was a man who had already spent years in prison and hadn't coped well with either imprisonment or freedom. He was also in a destructive relationship in which neither partner was content. Despite his objections, legal actions were undertaken both on his behalf and for those on Death Row elsewhere.

As he waited for dawn on the day of his death, Gilmore entertained family and friends in his cell and even spoke by telephone to his idol, country singer Johnny Cash.

When the first shafts of cold light broke through he was taken to the Cannery at Utah State Prison where he was strapped to an old office chair. A canvas bag was placed on his head and a paper target attached to his chest. The five anonymous members of the firing squad, selected from Utah's police force, were shielded from view by a curtain. Each policeman fired a single shot from a rifle after Gilmore uttered his famous line: 'Let's do it.'

Gilmore's body was immediately taken to hospital where transplantable organs were removed. There were four holes in the office chair. One member of the firing squad had been given a blank to safeguard the feelings of anyone who might regret their participation.

It was 19 years before the firing squad was again in action in Utah. This time convicted child killer, John Albert Taylor, who plumped for death by firing squad to cause maximum embarrassment to the state, was restrained in a specially-constructed chair.

One witness account, given by a radio station journalist, gives a graphic description of his death under fire.

> '[We] saw this very large man strapped to a chair. His eyes were darting back and forth. He was strapped to the chair by his hands and feet and lifted his chin for Warden Hank Galetka to secure a strap around his neck and place the black hood over his head. At 12:03 am, on the count of three, the five riflemen, standing 23 feet away, fired at a white cloth target pinned over Taylor's heart. Blood darkened the chest area of his navy blue clothing, and four minutes later a doctor pronounced him dead.'

Between these two killings, Romanian dictator Nicolae Ceausescu and his wife, Elena, were executed by machine gun on Christmas Day 1989 after a hastily convened military court found them guilty of crimes against the Romanian people.

In Guatemala the macabre spectacle of two condemned men being shot was televized in 1996, a move that surely speeded through the introduction of death by lethal injection two years later.

In Thailand a single executioner firing a semi-automatic weapon has dispatched those sentenced to death since 1935, replacing the practice of beheading. The prisoner was strapped to a pole and clutched flowers as a nod to the country's prevailing Buddhist beliefs. Prior to the shooting, the executioner traditionally sought forgiveness from his quarry. When the prisoner was judged to be dead, a monitor raised a red flag to stop the

At 12.03am, on the count of three, five riflemen standing 23 feet away fired at a white cloth target pinned over Taylor's heart. Blood darkened the chest area.

The execution of Nazi officer Alphons Klein in 1945 for the murder of 475 prisoners during World War 2

shooting. This somewhat ponderous ceremony was shown on television in 2001. Again, within two years the system was replaced with death by lethal injection. It's probably worth noting, though, that televising the death of a convict has never resulted in the abandonment of the death penalty.

A 1953 British Royal Commission into capital punishment decided: '[Firing squads] do not possess even the first requisite of an efficient method, the certainty of causing immediate death.'

HANGING

As masked guards hurled insults, cameras rolled and chaos raged without and within, tyrant Saddam Hussein dropped to his death through the trapdoor of the red metal gallows once used to kill his foes.

The place was Camp Justice, a former intelligence centre in north Baghdad. The date was 31 December 2006 – the start of the Muslim festival of Eid al-Adha, ironically associated with reconciliation rather than retribution. The time was 5.45 am in Baghdad. The former tyrant's executioners wore civilian clothes and black balaclavas, seeming more like terrorists than agents of the state.

Iraqi security chief, Mouwafak al-Rubaie, was one of the official witnesses who afterwards spoke to the press.

'They tied his hands behind his back and it was a little bit tight and I instructed the guard to loosen it up and they tied his legs and carried him up to the gallows in front of us.

'He went up and he was offered the hood but he turned it down. He said: "No, there's no need for that." '

After a black scarf was placed around his neck, the noose was put over his head and firmly drawn with the knot left lying on his left shoulder. A guard began reading the Muslim declaration of faith and Saddam responded with the words: 'La illaha ilallah was Muhammadu rasu Allah', which translates to 'There is no God but Allah and Muhammad is his messenger'.

According to al-Rubaie: 'He repeated this twice and then he went down in no time; it was so quick and totally painless; it was over in a second. There was no movement after that.'

A Chinese man is prepared for execution in Manchuria in 1935 for protesting against the Japanese invasion of that part of China

In some places his death brought jubilation. Shias, especially those who had lost relatives while Saddam was in power, celebrated in the streets. At other venues the mood was ominous. Some of those in Saddam's home region, who shared his Sunni faith, were especially aggrieved, believing him the victim of 'victor's justice' following a show trial. By nightfall 70 people had died in three separate car bomb attacks.

Hanging: A History

APART FROM IRAQ, hanging is still used today in Egypt, Jordan, Pakistan, Iran, Singapore and Japan where, characteristically, prisoners from death row are told the date and time of execution just a few hours before it takes place. Family and lawyers are informed afterwards.

There's a science behind hanging that was refined in the nineteenth century. British hangmen and others had been content with the 'short drop', a limited length of rope used in conjunction with a gallows and a horse and cart. With the noose in place the cart was driven off and the victim danced on the end of the rope, dying slowly by strangulation.

In 1871 executioner Thomas Marwood imported and refined the Irish notion of a 'long drop' in which the length of rope was calculated with the weight and height of the prisoner in mind. A brass eyelet replaced the cumbersome lynch knot and thus the prisoner died from a swift neck break rather than protracted asphyxiation. (It was occasionally necessary to dig a hole beneath the gallows to accommodate the required drop.) Problems only arose when the calculations went awry, which was when decapitations occurred. To prevent such disasters, the British published a table of weights and measures for hangmen, revised in 1913.

America, where hanging is still legal in two states, has generally favoured the standard drop, which aims for a securely broken neck.

In Iran, however, where executions are carried out in public, the tendency is to hoist up victims by the neck using cranes or gun barrels. Among those hanged in this manner are armed robbers and drug traffickers.

However long or short the drop, the rope needs to be boiled and stretched to remove elasticity. It's advisable for executioners to use soap or wax on the knot or brass eye to lubricate its action.

While conceding that capital punishment probably had not worked as a deterrent, British hangman Albert Pierrepoint declared in his biography: 'I operated, on behalf of the state, what I am convinced was the most humane and the most dignified method of meting out death to a delinquent – however justified or unjustified the allotment of death may be – and on behalf of humanity I trained other nations to adopt the British system of execution.'

As a method of capital punishment, hanging was backed by the UK's Royal Commission on Capital Punishment, which reported in 1953 that it held the advantage over the electric chair and the gas chamber. The Supreme Court of India has ruled that hanging is the least painful and most scientific method of execution.

Saddam was hanged following a trial at which he was found guilty of crimes against humanity. The charges against him related to reprisal killings he authorized following a botched assassination attempt in al-Dujail in 1982. Fearing further civil unrest with Saddam as its catalyst, the Iraqi government decided to go swiftly ahead with his execution, even before a trial to judge his responsibility for a chemical attack that killed thousands of Iraqi Kurds in 1988.

Iran and America were unlikely bedfellows in commending the execution. 'Today Saddam Hussein was executed after receiving a fair trial – the kind of justice he denied the victims of his brutal regime,' said US president George Bush. Other responses were more guarded and there was general discomfort at the speed of the execution, which followed an appeals process that was exhausted in just three weeks.

Nonetheless, hanging is one of the most enduring methods of capital punishment and as Saddam's death proved, one of the most effective. While there are horror stories about hangings that have gone wrong, most victims are dispatched at speed.

STONING

In May 2006 international reports claimed a man and a woman had been stoned to death in a cemetery in Iran. Abbas Hajizadeh and Mohboubeh Mohammadi had been found guilty of both murder and adultery but it was the second charge that was punishable by stoning under Islamic Sharia law.

The aftermath of a public stoning, in this case the gang of Bachha Sakoo, an Afghan bandit

Stoning is deemed appropriate for moral crimes and there are guidelines that apply. For adultery, the stones used should 'not be large enough to kill the person by one or two strikes; nor should they be so small that they could not be defined as stones'.

The sentence may follow a considerable spell in jail. Before it is carried out, the victim is washed and wrapped in white sheets or a shroud. Men are buried waist deep in the ground while the depth for women is to their

Stones used should not be large enough to kill the person by one or two strikes; nor should they be so small that they could not be defined as stones

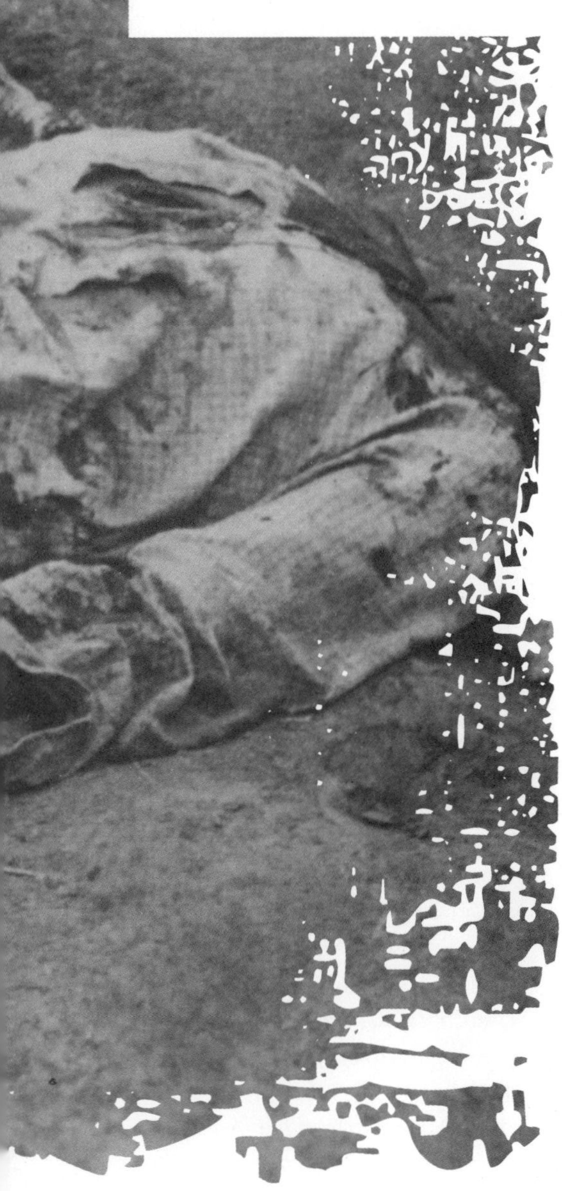

armpits or neck. Traditionally, relatives of the aggrieved cast the first stone although there's evidence it becomes a community event. Should detainees escape from their earthen confinement, it is held they should be freed. However, excitable crowds and guards may not allow that to happen. One woman, Zoleykhah Kadkhoda, was apparently revived at the morgue after she was stoned but her ultimate fate is unknown.

If the reports about stonings coming out of Iran are true then it brings to an end an apparent suspension of this archaic capital method. Iran's government came under pressure from the rest of the world after footage of stonings was circulated on the Internet, attracting fierce condemnation. Opponents point out it is women and the poor who are targeted through the system. According to Amnesty International, there may be up to nine women and two men currently under sentence of death by stoning in Iran.

While stoning is a feature of Sharia law it does not occur in all Islamic countries. There are sporadic reports of it happening in Saudi Arabia, Afghanistan and the United Arab Emirates. The sentence of stoning has also been handed down by Sharia courts in Nigeria, where about a third of the country adheres to strict Islamic law. However, Nigerian politicians insist those sentences are invariably overturned on appeal.

The execution of St Stephen in Jerusalem in around AD45 was by stoning

Historically, stoning has occurred not least because it is sanctioned in the Old Testament. One of the early Christian martyrs, St Stephen, was stoned to death. In medieval England there was also a sentence of pressing to death, where the victim was strapped to the ground and large boulders were piled upon him until he was crushed to death. It happened in America as well, in the wake of witch fever at Salem in 1692. Afterwards, the penalty was thought so barbaric it was outlawed.

LIFE ON DEATH ROW

In China the death penalty is generally carried out within seven days of sentencing. If a prisoner appeals against the sentence but is found guilty at a second trial, then execution is immediate. This means the burden of life without hope is eliminated for the convict and, of course, the financial burden upon the state of maintenance for a condemned man is removed.

However, death row exists in most other countries that retain the death penalty, a grim place where doomed convicts languish awaiting an execution date. The over-used description of them is 'dead men walking'. Legal systems are rightly thorough when it comes to a capital case and, in general, every avenue is explored. But this means that men and, to a much smaller extent, women are kept waiting in a protracted limbo between life and death.

Inmates on death rows across America can expect an early wake-up call at about 6.30 am, after which they will eat breakfast in their cells, where they also have their lunch and dinner. Meals are served on plastic plates and eaten with plastic utensils.

Personal decorations are generally not allowed in the cells, which are typically windowless. Each cell probably has a bed, steel sink and wall-mounted toilet and the only other furniture is likely to be a table fixed to the wall.

Prisoners are permitted televisions, radios and an ice chest but apart from watches and religious medals, personal effects are rarely allowed.

Work and recreation are limited, as is the opportunity for exercise, although prisoners are entitled to daily showers.

Countdown to death

A 1986 law improved conditions for the condemned, but perhaps the most numbing aspect of life on death row – the fact that one day's routine is identical to the next – remained the same. Only visits from family, friends or lawyers make a difference. And it is here that arrangements vary widely between prisons.

In New Jersey, where the last execution was in 1963, the rules are harsh and communication with anyone other than lawyers is severely limited. Inmates must sign up to use the single phone designated for personal calls and are limited to only 20 minutes talk time. Further, the prisoner may have no more than two visits a month from immediate relatives. Visits are limited to one hour and are non-contact. The only people inmates can meet without separation by a glass partition are other inmates, prison personnel, clergy and lawyers.

Meanwhile, at San Quentin, in California, where executions are more frequent, visits are hosted in small cubicles without partitions and can happen any day. Those families who have travelled a long distance benefit from extended hours, although violent prisoners are deprived of this perk.

Uniformly, when a death row inmate leaves the unit for any reason, he must wear both handcuffs and leg irons.

Some improvements have been needed to accommodate the ageing profile of death row inmates. Because inmates frequently spend a decade or two in these units, there are more death row residents aged over 60 than ever before. The effects of ageing are increasingly apparent and executing the elderly seems starkly uncivilized. 'Dead man walking is one thing,' said Jonathan Turley, a George Washington University law professor who has worked with older prisoners. 'Dead man being pushed along to the execution chamber in a wheelchair is another thing.'

According to some observers, progress in this area has not been sufficient. In his 1998 book, *Death Work: A Study of the Modern Execution Process*, Robert Johnson writes: 'With only rare exceptions, condemned prisoners are demoralized by their bleak confinement and defeated by the awesome prospect of death by execution. Worn down in small and almost imperceptible ways, they gradually become less than fully human. At the end the prisoners are helpless pawns in the modern execution drill. They give in, they give up and submit, yielding themselves to the execution team and the machinery of death.'

According to Willie Turner, who spent 17 years on death row in Virginia before his execution in 1995:

> **'It's the unending, uninterrupted immersion in death that wears on you so much. It's the parade of friends and acquaintances who leave for the death house and never come back while your own desperate and lonely time drains away. It's the boring routine of claustrophobic confinement, punctuated by eye-opening dates with death that you helplessly hope will be averted. It's watching yourself die over the years in the eyes of family and friends.'**

Not a single hour went by, he said, without contemplating his execution.

The devastating psychological effects brought about by years of hopeless incarceration has been termed 'death row syndrome' and those who suffer from it frequently choose death as an escape route.

The family of convicted murderer and Crips Gang founder Stanley Tookie Williams view his corpse after his execution by lethal injection in 2005

Delaying the hour

Serial killer Michael Ross was one hour away from execution by lethal injection in Connecticut in 2005 when a court stayed his execution after hearing he was possibly a victim of 'death row syndrome'.

Ross had waived his right to appeal but a court judge intervened when he heard about the potentially tormented mental state of the man who killed at least eight young women before his arrest in 1983.

Public defenders argued that the extreme conditions of isolation in a high-security prison essentially coerced him into dropping his appeals. A former deputy warden at the super-maximum-security Connecticut prison where Ross was confined described the environment as similar to 'living in a submarine or cave.'

Dr. Stuart Grassian, an expert on death row inmates, wrote in court papers: 'The conditions of confinement are so oppressive, the helplessness endured in the roller coaster of hope and despair so wrenching and exhausting, that ultimately the inmate can no longer bear it, and then it is only in dropping his appeals that he has any sense of control over his fate.'

Eventually the execution was delayed until a court-appointed expert could decide whether Ross was competent to make life-or-death decisions. Ross, who had attempted suicide three times during 17 years on death row, finally had his way. On 13 May 2005 he died in the first execution carried out in Connecticut in 45 years.

The only other punctuation in routine a death row inmate can expect is the execution of fellow inmates, occasions usually marked by cat-calling, hymn-singing or, sometimes, dead silence.

In Missouri, death row has been eradicated and its residents are streamed with other prisoners, helping reduce the psychological impact of segregation.

Despite this sterile existence there have been examples of prisoners enriched by their life on Death Row. Inevitably, this has come about through the abundant time available for contemplation and the availability of books.

One such example is Stanley 'Tookie' Williams, bodybuilder and a co-founder of the notorious Crips gang in south central Los Angeles. In 1981 he was found guilty of four cold-blooded murders and given the death penalty. At first his prison record entirely supported the notion that he was a violent 'no-hoper'. After a succession of vicious fights

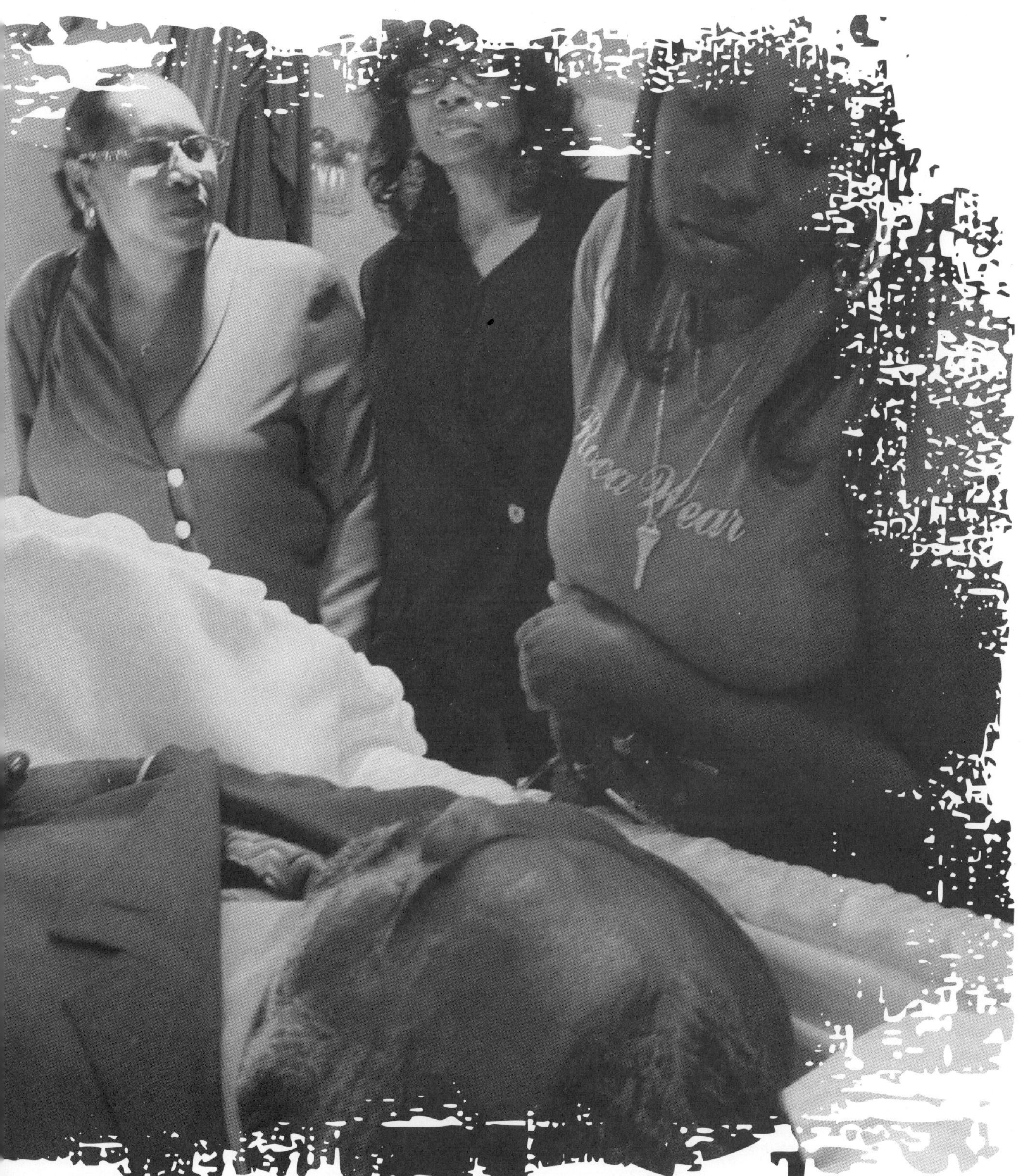

with guards and fellow prisoners he spent long spells in solitary.

But from 1993 he began issuing a succession of anti-gang sentiments that did much work for youth re-education, He co-wrote children's books and even attracted a handful of nominations for the Nobel Peace Prize as well as a number of literary prizes. A film about his life was made and aptly titled *Redemption*.

'It was during a seven-year stint in solitary confinement where I was able to battle my demons and re-educate myself and embrace edification and spiritual cultivation and that's

A photo of Karla Faye Tucker as she awaited execution on death row in Texas for the 1983 murder of a local man with a pickaxe

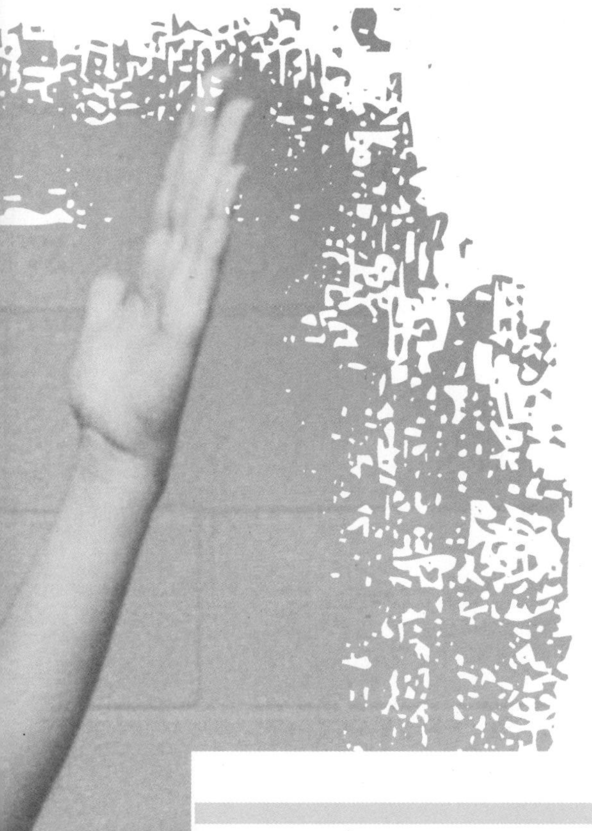

where I was able to develop a sense of redemption,' Williams once explained.

However, none of this was enough to win him a reprieve. Despite a petition of some 175,000 names, California governor Arnold Schwarzenegger refused clemency. Williams died in Marin County in 2005 from a lethal injection, having renounced his former life but without informing on former colleagues to police. Until the end he protested his innocence. His incarceration on death row lasted no less than 24 years.

Time on death row is usually marked by endless rounds of legal hearings intended to overturn the punishment. But while inmates may be buoyed when a judge finds in their favour they can be devastated when prosecutors are able, through the courts, to have the ruling overturned and the punishment re-instated.

Convicted killer Karla Faye Tucker Brown

'I didn't care about anybody. I didn't place any value on myself or anybody else.'

had exhausted all other options when she made an appeal for clemency to George W Bush, then governor of Texas, asking him to commute her capital sentence to life in jail.

Tucker Brown, a self-confessed 'needle freak', turned to murder after a three-day orgy of drink, drugs and sex. She and a drug-dealer boyfriend killed for kicks when they bludgeoned two people to death. Years later she told TV show host Larry King, via a taped interview: 'I didn't care about anybody. I didn't place any value on myself or anybody else.'

During her spell on death row she discovered a strong faith and married (by proxy) prison chaplain Dana Lane Brown. Her case – that a drug-addled prostitute had behind bars evolved into a compassionate born-again Christian – won support from across America and around the world. Like Williams, it was generally agreed that she posed no further threat to society. But Bush turned down her appeal and Tucker Brown died by lethal injection on 3 February 1998, the first women to be executed in Texas since the US Civil War.

Wrongfully on the row

There has been a series of well-documented cases about innocent men being freed from death row, a number which has increased due to advances in DNA testing.

One such example is Ryan Matthews, who was 17 when he was said to have been involved in the killing of a grocer. An alleged accomplice implicated Matthews and in 1999 he was given the death penalty after being positively identified by witnesses. However, after five years on death row the DNA on a ski mask used in the crime was found to belong to another man – who had bragged about committing the murder when he was in jail on other charges.

When the Louisiana Supreme Court ordered a re-trial, prosecutors realized there was no evidence to connect Matthews to the scene of the crime and declined to go ahead with another hearing. In 2004 he was a free man. Matthews became the 14th person in the US to be freed from death row after post-conviction DNA testing.

Trial blunders are also a cause for concern. In 2004 Ernest Ray Willis was freed from death row, 18 years after his conviction for the murder by arson of two women in Iraan, Texas.

Willis, an unemployed oilfield worker, was given anti-psychotic drugs in jail prior to court appearances, the effects of which haunted him after prosecutors construed them as a symptom of remorselessness. The drugs also rendered him unable to assist his defence attorney. In 2000 Judge M Brock Jones ruled there had been problems with the trial and it wasn't until four years later that US District Judge Royal Furgeson threw out the conviction, citing the needless drugging. He was also concerned that the prosecution suppressed a report by a psychologist claiming Willis was not a dangerous person. If those reasons were not sufficient to upend the conviction the fact that the fire was now thought to be caused by an electrical fault surely was.

Some prosecutors, to secure a conviction, have clearly over-reached and attempted to send men to their deaths on improperly tested evidence.

More troubling still are instances of convictions that occur when a confession to the crime has already been made. Rolando Cruz and Alesandro Hernandez were sentenced to death for a child killing even when another felon, Brian Dugan, had already admitted to it. As they languished behind bars for a crime they didn't commit, Dugan was freed and murdered a seven-year-old girl.

There have been cases of prisoners being exonerated after the intervention of journalism students who were able to carry out a more

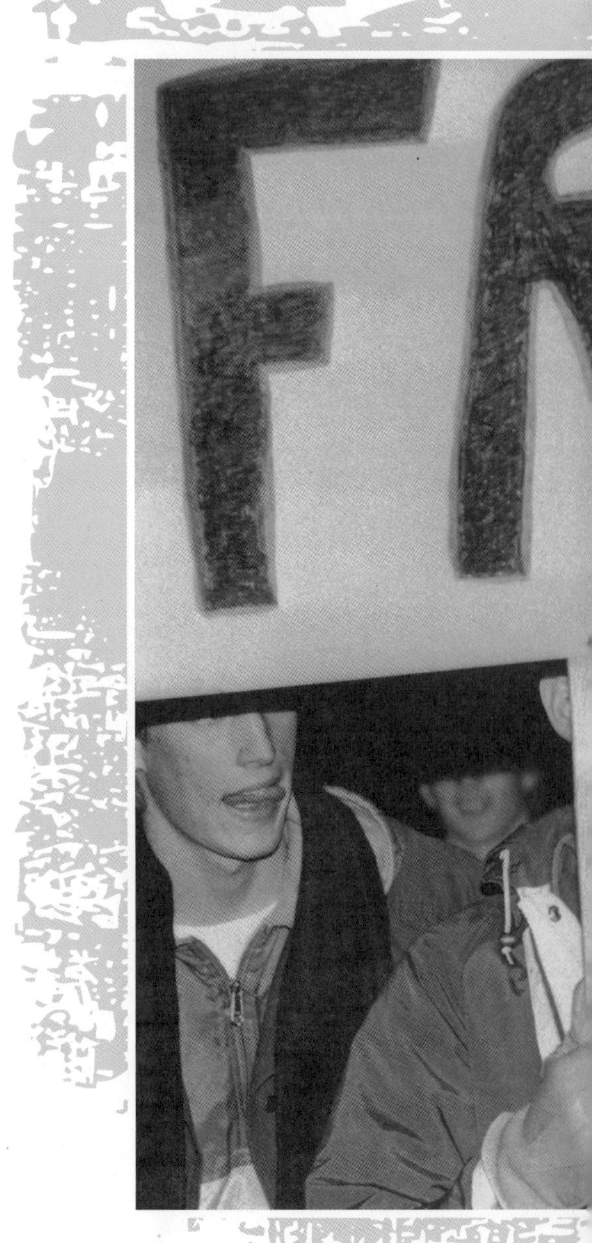

exacting investigation than the police or the defence team at the time of the trial.

Innocence projects run by volunteers and students have sprung up across America in an effort to secure justice for those apparently badly served by the system. They enjoy a sound success rate but are short on resources.

Final hours

An insight into the last hours of a condemned man comes from the rigid routine of Huntsville Maximum Security jail in Texas, the home of America's busiest death chamber where lethal injection is the procedure of choice.

The prisoner is transported to Huntsville from the prison's death row, which is actually at a different unit some 20 miles distant, in the early afternoon. As he has lived elsewhere, the prisoner will not know any of the men responsible for his execution. His destination is one of eight cells next to the death chamber where he goes, generally, in the company of the prison chaplain.

At 2 pm the condemned man is permitted his final telephone call. An hour later it's time for a last visit with family members, friends or

In 1986 pro-death penalty protesters make their point outside South Carolina's Central Correctional Institution while awaiting the execution of double-murderer James Terry Roach

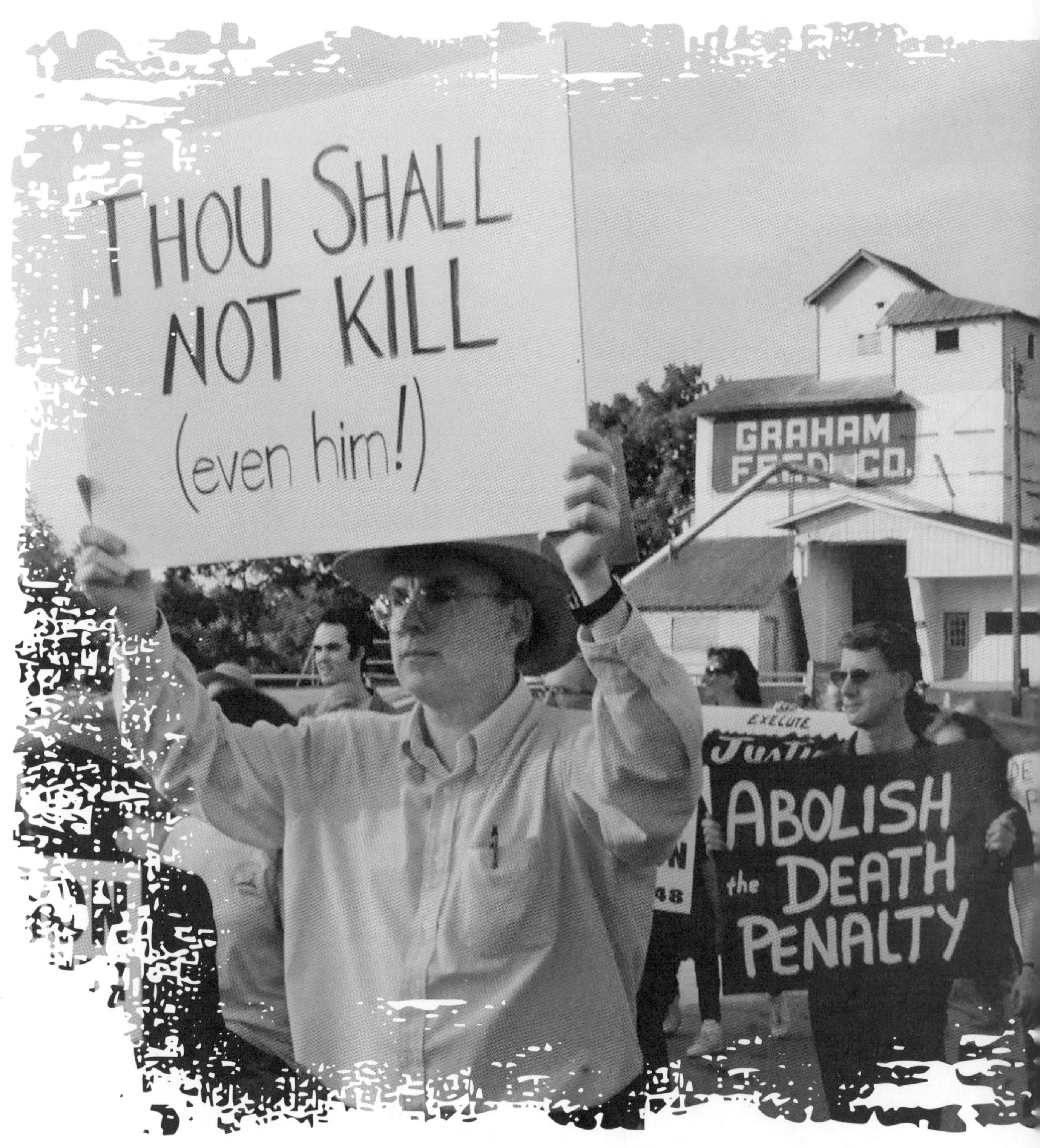

In 2001 anti-death penalty protesters marched through Indiana to object to the execution of Timothy McVeigh, the Oklahoma city bomber

supporters. Then, at 4.30 pm he has his final meal.

Nothing will happen until a call comes to the chief warden from the governor's office, giving the go-ahead for the execution. Once, prisoners might have invested hope in getting a last-minute stay of execution that would have delayed their final hour. In fact, in 2003 the number of interventions by the Supreme Court fell to just over 3 per cent of applications received, a rate some 20 per cent less than a decade earlier.

It's usually around 6 pm that the final process swings into motion. The prisoner is not usually handcuffed or chained when he is taken from his cell through the grey door of the blue-walled death chamber to an awaiting gurney. Most prisoners are co-operative.

Those that refuse to come willingly undergo the trauma of a forcible 'cell extraction' by guards wearing face shields and body armour.

On hand is a 'tie down' team of five people whose job is to strap the prisoner to the gurney, a well-practised procedure that only takes about half a minute. Many prisoners at this point utter 'thank you' as they are fixed into a horizontal crucifixion pose before the tie down team withdraws. A white sheet is usually pulled up to the chin of the victim, although the outline of the seven mustard leather straps and their silver buckles can still be seen beneath.

Now it's the turn of a two-man medical team to insert the necessary tubes used to administer the fatal doses.

Witnesses gathered for the execution are ushered into a neighbouring, windowed room. There is a maximum of sixteen witnesses, five each for the prisoner, the family of his or her victims and the media plus the prisoner's religious advisor. They watch as a microphone on a boom comes down from the ceiling to amplify the condemned man's final statement. After his words have died away the warden gives a signal for the lethal injection process to begin. (Before his retirement, warden Jim Willett raised his glasses to indicate readiness.) In some states there is a lethal injection machine so that no one need feel responsible for actually administering death, but in Texas the task remains in human hands.

A doctor is on hand to pronounce death. The dead body is then transferred to a funeral home gurney. If the prisoner is too poor to pay for a funeral he is buried by fellow inmates in a prison cemetery, in a grave marked by his prison number. Warden Willett made it his business to attend when the dead prisoner had no family.

The effect on witnesses can be profound. Leigh Anne Gideon, a former reporter and execution veteran, explained in a radio documentary: 'You'll never hear another sound like a mother wailing whenever she is watching her son be executed. There's no other sound like it. It is just this horrendous wail. You can't get away from it. That wail surrounds the room. It's definitely something you won't ever forget.'

As for the journalists themselves, they must decide whether they are serving the greater good. Wayne Sorge, news director of KSAM in Huntsville, Texas, has justified his presence on numerous occasions.

> 'I wrestle with myself about the fact that it's easier now, and was I right to make part of my income from watching people die.

Food is basic in jail – and ranges in quality widely from prison to prison

And I have to recognize the fact that what I do for a living is hold up a mirror to people of what their world is. Capital punishment is part of that, and if you are in the city where more capital punishment occurs than any place else in the civilized world, that's got to be part of the job.'

Outside the prison there is frequently a sizeable crowd of people. It is generally divided into two distinct camps: those supporting the death penalty and those opposed to it. In a land that prides itself on its freedom to speak, they will continue to attend.

Time of death

The timings may vary – some prisons choose midnight as the execution hour – and the details can change but the grim outcome is the same. In some US jails other prisoners are uncomfortably close to the site of the death chamber and that casts a pall of gloom over the relevant prison wing.

Keeping death row prisoners near to the place of execution occurs in other countries, too. When British citizen Mirza Tahir Hussain was condemned to death in Pakistan, he was kept within earshot of the prison gallows.

'[On death row] you can hear the guards and all the officials gathering for that purpose; when the condemned is made to stand on the

Last Meals

Traditionally, the fodder served to a condemned man is his choice and it can range from nothing to a lavish spread.

- **Oliver David Cruz**, a rapist and murderer put to death in Texas in August 2000, ordered spicy beef fajitas, beans and rice, flour tortillas, onions, tomatoes, avocados, a banana split and an orange juice.

- In September 2002 **Ron Shamburger**, who killed a fellow student during a burglary, asked for nachos with chili and cheese, a bowl of sliced jalapeno peppers, a bowl of piquant sauce, two sliced and grilled onions, salad and some toasted tortilla chips.

- Child killer **James Powell**, executed in October 2002, requested only a pot of coffee.

- In November 2002 **William Chappell**, at 66 the oldest man ever executed in Texas, asked for the same meal served to other offenders that day. He had been convicted of a triple murder.

- Before his death in Texas on 8 March 2005 convicted hitman **George Hopper** asked for six eggs over easy, 10 biscuits, 12 pieces of bacon, a bowl of grits, a bowl of thick white gravy, strawberry preserve, fried chicken, French Fries and chocolate meringue pie.

- When **John B Nixon, Snr** was put to death in Mississippi on 14 December 2005 at the age of 77, he had eaten a T-bone steak, buttered asparagus spears, a baked potato with soured cream, peach pie, vanilla ice cream and sweet tea.

- **Shawn Paul Humphries** plumped for a McDonalds, fries, broccoli with cheese and oat cereal, washed down with a Dr Pepper before his execution on 2 December 2005, in South Carolina.

- **Jay Wesley Neill**, who killed four in a bank robbery in 1984, ate a double cheeseburger, fries, peach and cherry cobbler and a pint of vanilla ice cream, washed down with a large bottle of fruit juice before his death on 12 December 2002, in Oklahoma.

- **Anthony Johnson**, executed in Alabama on the same day as Neill, requested a sandwich from the prison vending machine.

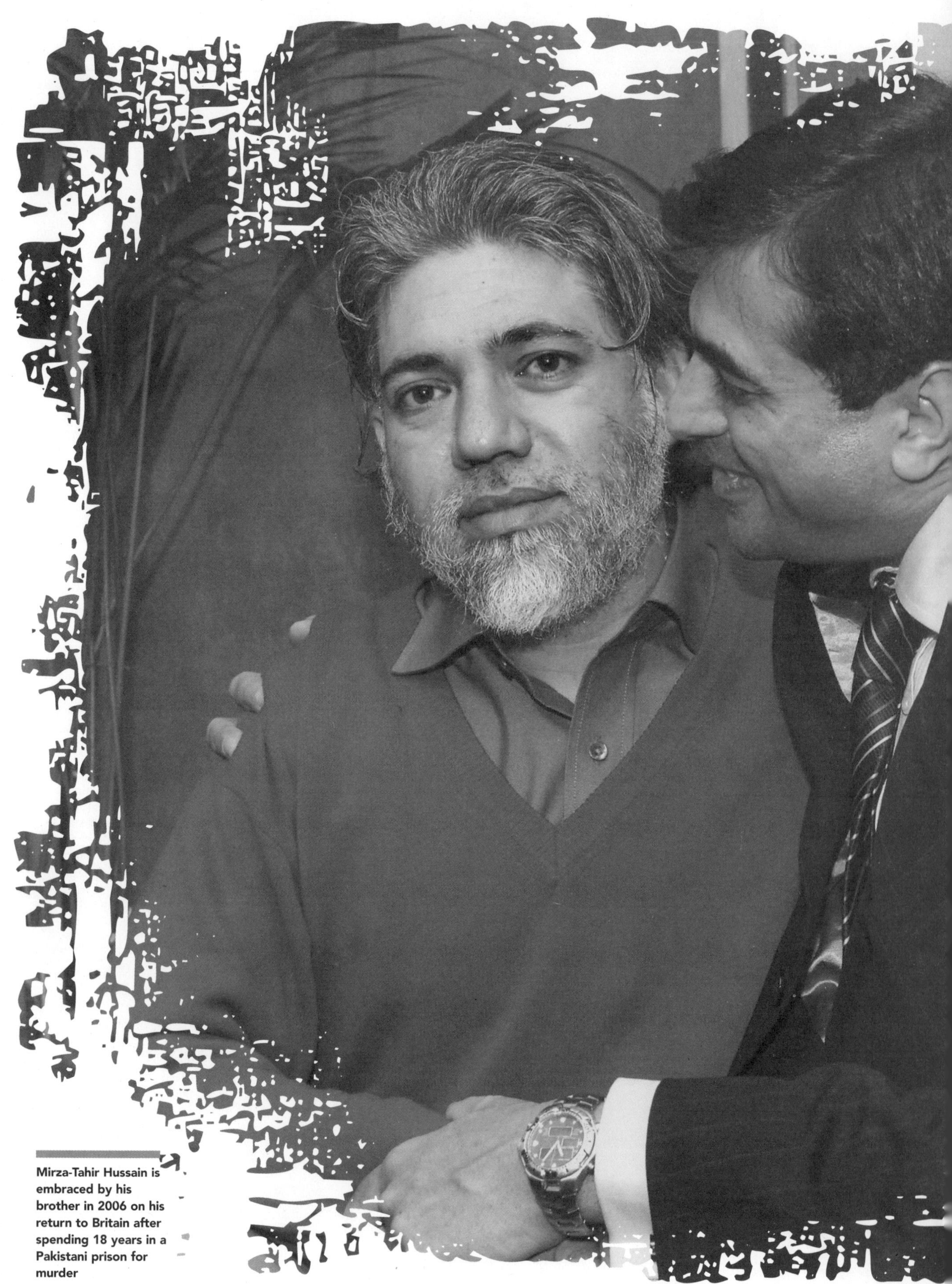

Mirza-Tahir Hussain is embraced by his brother in 2006 on his return to Britain after spending 18 years in a Pakistani prison for murder

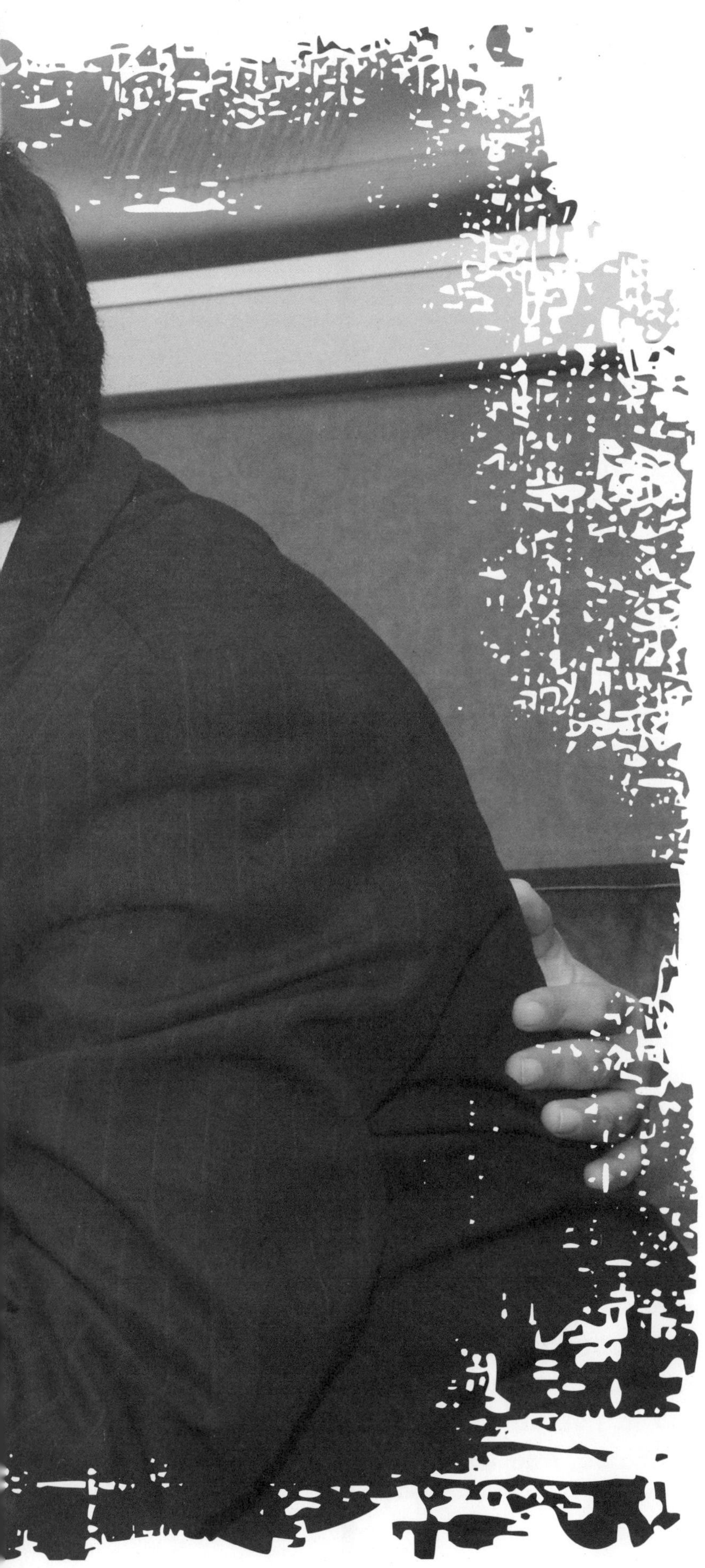

trap door, and when the trap door opens, and when he is hanged. You can hear all that,' Mr Hussain told the BBC's Asian Network, clearly distressed by the ordeal.

Hussain was freed 18 years after a driver was killed in a scuffle, apparently having threatened the British student. Although he was pronounced not guilty of murder in Pakistan's regular court, Hussain was condemned to death by a majority decision in a Sharia court. He endured the torment of four stays of execution before being freed by Pakistan's President Musharaf following representations from, among others, Prince Charles and Prime Minister Tony Blair.

After one such episode he confessed to a journalist:

> 'I'm looking forward to ending the whole thing one way or another. Mentally one reaches such a state that we need some decisions.'

Hussain was one of 484 condemned men at the jail in Rawalpindi, where the total prison population was 5,200. He shared a cell measuring 12 ft by eight ft with two other men.

In 2005 at least 2,148 people were executed in 22 countries. In the same year more than five thousand people were sentenced to death. The vast majority of executions – 94 per cent – occur in just four countries: China, Iran, Saudi Arabia and the USA. In China, the number of executions is judged a state secret and it is thought the real figure could be much higher than that ascertained from official sources. One Chinese lawyer has estimated that as many as eight thousand people were condemned and executed there during that period.

According to latest figures, over half the countries of the world have abolished the death penalty in law or practice. Portugal stands out for having carried out its last execution in 1849. For most countries, however, the move away from capital punishment came in the latter half of the twentieth century. Although 68 countries retain the death penalty it has not been carried out in most on a regular – or even annual – basis.

...On Pain of Death

'I've lived a pathetic life, and I believe it was education that helped me to change. It was through education that I was able to create common sense and use reasoning. And it was through this that I developed a conscience that led to my redemption.

'This is something I feel I was obligated to do as a man, period – to do something that would help the youth out there. I feel obligated to try to convince them that the life that they wanted to live or are thinking about living – the so-called thug life, or the gang life, or the criminal life, or the drug life – will ruin their lives forever. I was motivated to do something in my small way – to make a contribution.'

— Stan 'Tookie' Williams

'Technology has come a long way since the electric chair. Because an injection is less painful and less offensive it would be foolish not to use it.'

— Massachusetts State Senator Edward Kirby

'It is curious, but 'til that moment I had never realized what it means to destroy a healthy, conscious man. When I saw the prisoner step aside to avoid the puddle, I saw the mystery, the unspeakable wrongness, of cutting a life short when it is in full tide. This man was not dying, he was alive just as we were alive. All the organs of his body were working – bowels digesting food, skin renewing itself, nails growing, tissues forming – all toiling away in solemn foolery. His nails would still be growing when he stood on the drop, when he was falling through the air with a tenth of a second to live. His eyes saw the yellow gravel and the grey walls, and his brain still remembered, foresaw, reasoned – reasoned even about puddles. He and we were a party of men walking together, seeing, hearing, feeling, understanding the same world; and in two minutes, with a sudden snap, one of us would be gone – one mind less, one world less.'

— George Orwell discussing a hanging he witnessed in India in 1931

'People who are sure about the death penalty, one way or the other, must have greater insight than me.'

— Huntsville Prison Warden Jim Willet (retired).

'However horrible the act they have committed, I believe that everyone has the potential to improve and correct themselves. Therefore, I am optimistic that it remains possible to deter criminal activity, and prevent such harmful consequences of such acts in society, without having to resort to the death penalty.'

— Dalai Lama

'The art of policing is, in order not to punish often, to punish severely.'

— Napoleon

'A system that will take life must first give justice.'

— Former American Bar Association President John J. Curtin, Jr.

'While there are logical arguments in favor of the death penalty in theory, capital punishment does not exist in theory. The reality of the death penalty, as it is practiced in the real world, makes it a nonsustainable criminal-justice policy.'

— Matthew Robinson, Associate Professor of Criminal Justice at Appalachian State University

'I knew my objective was a state-assisted suicide and when it happens it's "in your face, motherf——s". You just did something you're trying to say should be illegal for medical personnel.'

— Oklahoma Bomber Timothy McVeigh, executed 2001

'Revenge is a kind of wild justice, which the more man's nature runs to, the more ought law to weed it out.'

— Francis Bacon

'If we execute murderers and there is in fact no deterrent effect, we have killed a bunch of murderers. If we fail to execute murderers, and doing so would in fact have deterred other murders, we have allowed the killing of a bunch of innocent victims. I would much rather risk the former. This, to me, is not a tough call.

— John McAdams, Marquette University Department of Political Science, on deterrence

An inmate of a Filipino prison sings a traditional pabasa hymn during Lent

CONCLUSION

More than nine million people are living behind bars in over 200 different countries around the globe, the majority as pre-trial detainees.

The three countries with the biggest jail populations – the US, China and Russia – account for more than half the world's prisoners. But it is not just in these countries that the number of jail birds is on the up. Three-quarters of the countries that took part in the World Prison Population List reported an increase in their prison populations.

No one knows why the rates are climbing. America is conducting a war against drug offenders while, from time to time, China cracks down on political dissidents, pushing up the head count in the country's prisons. Iraq is processing more prisoners than it might normally expect to due to its civil unrest. But the hike in numbers is registering across the board, with no single reason upon which to attach blame.

As no one wants to live next door to those branded a danger to society, jails will be with us for the foreseeable future. Derisory sentences are more likely to keep us awake at night than the discomfort of prisoners crammed together in unsanitary conditions. Also, nobody much cares about the finer feelings of those on the inside when they themselves failed to show one iota of sensitivity while they were free.

There are plenty of reformed characters out there, those who've been behind bars, paid their debt to society and resolved never to return to prison again. So in some instances prison works as we hope it should. But perhaps the grim experience of being inside does lie at the root of the problem of bulging prisons.

For despite everything that has been learned about incarceration during its history, ancient and modern, prisons seem to satisfy only one single issue: keeping criminals off the streets. It's a policy that's hard to resist but it seems certain that some tweaking is needed to a system that might otherwise collapse under its own weight.

Re-offending is a perennial problem and if a solution to the 'revolving door' types could be found – offenders who often spend longer inside prison than they do outside – the prison population would be significantly lower.

Re-offending is a young man's game. By the time inmates pass the age of 50 fewer than two per cent will return to prison. When it comes to the ageing prison population a different consideration causes prison authorities to think – the soaring costs of health care.

A handful of prisons have been opened devoted entirely to these 'grey' convicts, who more often require a wheelchair, IV drip or the contents of a well-stocked pharmacy than barbed wire or well-armed guards.

The prison system as it stands, tough on crime and unbending in its desire to cage wrongdoers, throws up another area of concern. Even those who respond badly to Spartan or barbarous conditions behind bars are likely one day to be released among us. If they have been brutalized they will become brutal, even after they re-join the ranks of society. Then the result of deficiencies in the prison system falls very much into our laps.

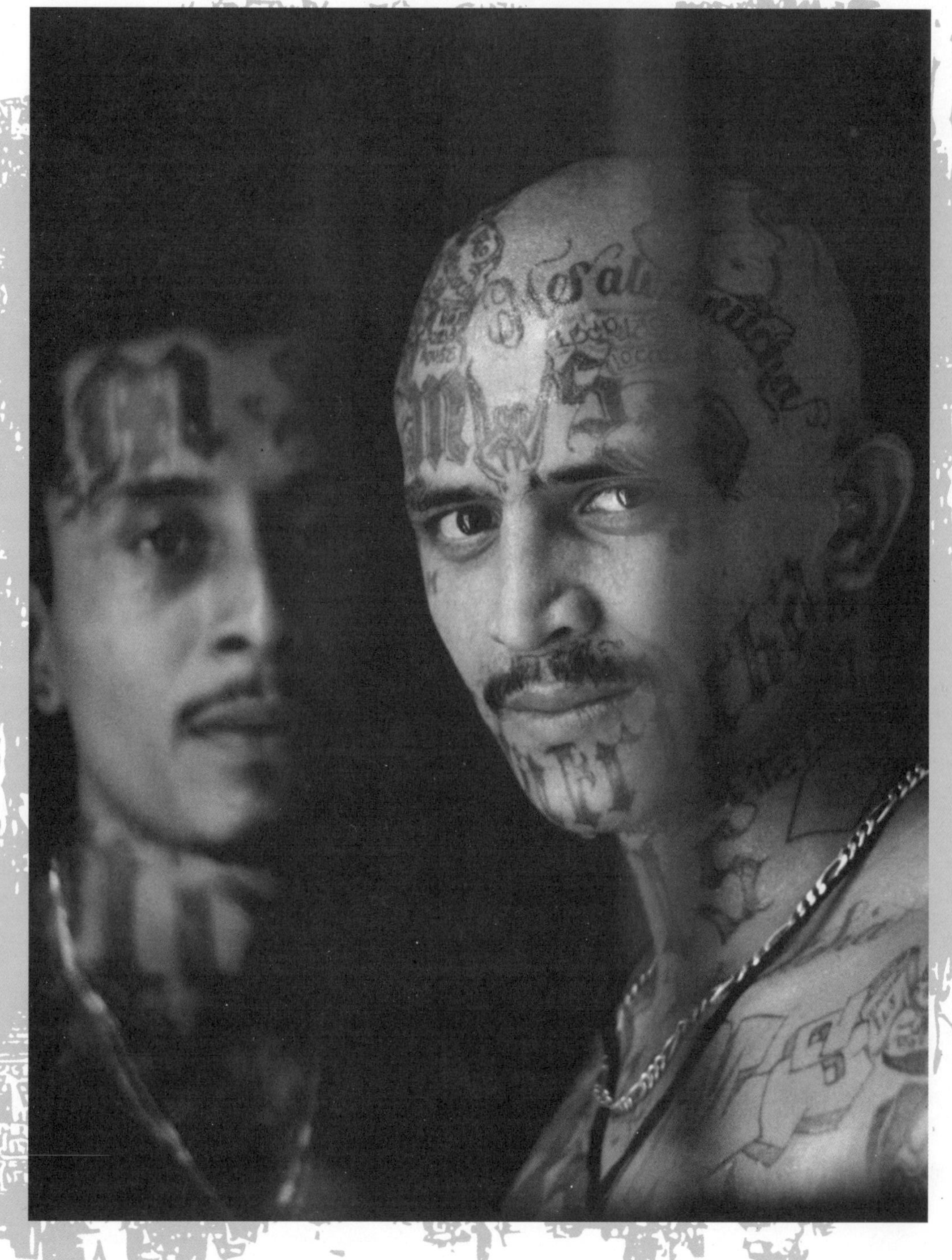

Index

Picture Credits

Corbis 16, 18, 20, 22, 23, 24, 26, 32, 34, 36, 38, 42, 44, 48, 51, 54, 58, 61, 62, 64, 66, 68 both, 72, 74, 76, 80, 82, 84, 88, 90, 92, 94, 96, 100, 102, 106, 113, 114, 118, 122, 124, 132, 135, 138, 140, 144, 146, 147, 150, 152, 154, 156, 160, 162, 164, 168, 172, 173, 174, 178, 181, 182, 184, 185, 186, 190, 194, 196, 198, 204, 206 (© Christian Poveda/Corbis)

PA Photos 78, 96, 109, 111, 120, 126, 192

Getty 48, 56, 86, 104, 200

Kobal 148

Flickr 129 (Flickrname: 'Msunderstood299'), 136 (Flickrname: Larry Halff)